Elementary Price Theory

Elementary Price Theory

Peter C. Dooley
UNIVERSITY OF SASKATCHEWAN

NEW YORK
Appleton-Century-Crofts
EDUCATIONAL DIVISION

Meredith Corporation

Copyright © 1967 by
MEREDITH PUBLISHING COMPANY

6128-4

Library of Congress Card Number: 67-13465

PRINTED IN THE UNITED STATES OF AMERICA

390-27063-6

PREFACE

Elementary Price Theory was written for beginning students who so often find price theory the most difficult and the least useful part of economics. It is the purpose of this book to make the subject understandable and to show that it is relevant.

Most of the book is devoted to purely theoretical topics, which are developed as simply and as orderly as possible without sacrificing accuracy. No attempt has been made to prove every proposition mentioned nor to mention every proposition which exists in the field. The book emphasizes the main outline of conventional partial equilibrium analysis. The theories of consumer demand, production and cost, and market structures are used to explain price determination in the product market; and the theories of factor supply and marginal productivity are used to explain income distribution in the factor market.

For the beginning student, theory alone is not enough—it is not evident to even good students that the theory is relevant. For this reason the last part of many chapters discusses the significance of the theory. These sections may be omitted without detracting from the development of the theory in subsequent chapters. Since beginning courses typically introduce the student to a wide range of microeconomic subjects—such as labor problems and farm problems—in addition to covering economic theory, a course in which this book is used may well be improved if it is supplemented with additional reading material on special topics. *Elementary Price Theory* may also be used as a supplement to one of the larger, more comprehensive textbooks.

The writer is indebted to several people who helped in the preparation of this book. Edward Budd was particularly generous with his time and spent many hours reading the manuscript. His instructive criticism on both the general outline and on specific passages improved the book in many ways. James Herendeen read an early draft of the book and made a number of suggestions which have been incorporated into this revision. Howard Sherman noted a number of weaknesses in an early draft, which the writer has tried to correct. Any faults which remain are due to the imperfect knowledge or to the curious preferences of the writer.

P.C.D.

CONTENTS

Elementary Price Theory

Introduction

What Is Price Theory?

A private enterprise economy, such as that of the United States, depends upon the market mechanism to channel its available resources into the production of the goods and services that consumers want. The market coordinates the mass of productive resources—oil pools and iron fields, machinists and merchants, bulldozers and stamping mills—with the maze of consumer wants—dish towels and window glass, oysters and potatoes, legal services and ocean voyages. It operates according to the rule, production for a profit. Those wants for which consumers are willing to pay the most are satisfied first, and those resources which yield the greatest revenues are used first.

Price theory explains how the human and natural resources of an economy are allocated in the production and distribution of goods and services. Every society has limited resources, but unlimited uses for resources. This relative scarcity raises a number of fundamental questions. (1) What will be produced? Will resources go into automobiles, skyscrapers, or rockets? That is, what quantity and quality of goods and services will be produced? Will there be a thousand or a million new houses? what kind? (2) How will goods be produced? Will a factory use hand-operated or automatic machinery? And, (3) for whom will goods be produced? How will the total output be divided? Will laborers or property owners get the larger share? These are questions with which price theory deals.

Prices help direct the allocation of resources. If two goods satisfy the same want or requirement equally well but sell at different prices, buyers will tend to purchase the less expensive good. For example, if a businessman finds that it is cheaper to make out his payroll with a computer than with a staff of bookkeepers, he will tend to buy the computer. Similarly, if a customer in a restaurant would be as satisfied with a hot dog as with a hamburger and if hot dogs cost 15 cents while hamburgers cost 25 cents, he will buy the hot dog. In both cases the principle is the same. *Relative prices*—the price of computers relative to the price of bookkeepers and the price of hot dogs relative to the price of hamburgers—determine what will be bought. The businessman *economizes* when he buys the services of the computer, and the restaurant customer *economizes* when he buys the hot dog.

Why Study Price Theory?

Most of us spend a good part of our lives engaged in economic activity. Many people spend more time performing economic functions than they spend doing anything else—with the possible exception of sleeping. Working, buying, planning, indeed, even sleeping have their economic aspects. For this reason, most of us think we know something about economics. Economics should be obvious, but it is not. An economy is one of the most complex phenomena known to man.

A knowledge of price theory will not make you rich, though it may help you get rich; a knowledge of price theory will not make you wise, though it may add to your wisdom. Price theory is a tool which can be used for many things. It is a tool that sees beneath the surface of economic activity and isolates the forces which operate on markets, just as an X-ray machine is a tool that sees beneath the skin and pictures what goes on below.

Price theory lies at the heart of many ideological and political conflicts. The chief differences between the economies of the Soviet Union and the United States are the institutions which are used to plan and direct production. In the USSR the questions of what, how, and for whom are mainly decided by the state, while in the USA they are partly decided by the market and partly decided by the state. The U.S. economy is called a *mixed economy* because it is governed by both public and private decisions.

When Congress considers labor, tariff, farm, and social welfare legislation, it is concerned with the operation of the price system. Should labor be allowed to organize and bargain as a unit in the market? Should certain businesses be subsidized by the taxing of competing imports? Should farmers get price supports? Should the poor be fed, housed, and clothed by the state? Price theory does not answer such questions, but it does provide useful tools to analyze them.

The Institutional Setting

Price theory developed historically to explain how resources are allocated in a capitalistic economy. It is conceivable that a price system could work effectively under a different set of institutions, but this book will be concerned with capitalism, based on private property, free contract, free markets, and production for a profit.

Capitalism is called a "private enterprise" or "free enterprise" system. The modifiers "private" and "free" refer to the institutions of private property and free contract. Under such a system production is undertaken for a profit by private enterprises, which are free to manage their own affairs and free to make contracts to buy and sell goods and services in the market.

The owner of private property has the right to exclude others from his property. As a general rule, he has the right to use or abuse his property as he pleases. The state enforces this right with its police and its courts. Trespassing laws and patent laws prevent others from using his property, laws which permit civil suits prevent others from abusing it, and laws against theft prevent others from taking it. However, property rights are not absolute rights, and they have changed over time. Many cities have zoning ordinances which restrict commercial and industrial properties to one part of the town and reserve another part of the town for residences. The Civil Rights Act of 1964 makes it illegal for an interstate business to exclude anyone from its premises on the basis of race, religion, or national origin. Traditionally, minors have not been allowed to exercise property rights without supervision, and in the past women's property rights were severely restricted.

For most purposes two parties are free to make any contract they wish, to specify any terms they wish, and the state will enforce it. A landlord, for example, can hold his tenant to a lease which requires the tenant to pay three times the going rent and to pay it a year in advance, provided the tenant originally agreed to such terms. If the tenant were to refuse to abide by the contract, the landlord could take him to court; and, if the court sided with the landlord, it could order the tenant to pay damages, to accept the terms of the contract, or stand in contempt of court. The last might carry a jail term. However, relatively few contracts are disputed and fewer still end in a court proceeding.

Frequently the terms of contracts are accepted as a matter of custom. The American supermarket typically operates under a single price system and sells on cash-and-carry terms, that is, goods are priced as marked, are paid for in cash, and are not delivered. Not too many years ago grocery shoppers expected to higgle over prices, to buy on credit, and to have their purchases delivered.

Custom in the form of common law has restricted the institution of free contract to certain rules. To illustrate, agreements which have been entered into fraudulently, or under duress, or with minors, are often not enforced by the state. In Europe during the Middle Ages custom restricted the right of contract so severely that it hardly existed for most economic relationships. Both lord and peasant were held to actions to which neither originally agreed and which neither could easily change. Peasants sometimes had the right of gleanage, that is, the right to pick over fields after the harvest and to keep what they gathered. The same peasant might be subject to the banality of grinding that grain at his lord's mill.

Today, legislatures have placed much of common law on the statute books, and, in addition, they have passed many other laws which limit contracts. For example, the Thirteenth Amendment prohibits anyone from being sold into slavery. In New York City the rent on many apartments has a legal maximum. The Sherman

Antitrust Act of 1890 provides that "Every contract, combination in the form of trust or otherwise, or conspiracy, in restraint of trade or commerce . . . is hereby declared to be illegal."

In a capitalistic economy private enterprises produce for a profit. Profit—the excess of revenues over costs—is the stimulus which draws forth and channels the production of goods and services. It induces businessmen to produce what people want to buy. A sales boom in motorcycles increases the profits that can be earned in their production and distribution. It is the prospect of higher profits which entices manufacturers to buy more materials, to employ more men, and to produce greater quantities and which also persuades retailers to stock, display, and sell more motorcycles.

A system of production for a profit, free exchange, and private property cannot exist without markets. Property is exchanged in markets, labor services are sold in markets, and profits are made in markets. In general, markets exist whenever and wherever buyers and sellers transact business; yet particular markets are not easily defined, because they may have no definite limits. They may be primarily local, as in the case of the market for retail groceries or automobile repairs. They may be regional, as in the case of the wholesale markets for beer and bricks. They may be national or international, as in the case of wheat or copper. Markets may cover a single identifiable product, such as grade A milk; or they may cover ɔ range of related products, such as dairy products.

The Circular Flow of Goods and Services

Our high standard of living, perhaps the chief benefit of our industrial civilization, is associated with an extensive division of labor. The modern man, farmer and urban dweller alike, consumes goods and services that are almost entirely produced by others. His food, his clothing, his every need is purchased in the market. He earns his income by selling his specialty in the market. In contrast, the subsistence farm families of the American frontier were practically self-sufficient. They grew their own food, spun their own thread, wove their own cloth, made their own clothing, and fell the lumber or cut the sod to make their own houses. They purchased relatively little from others. For the subsistence farmer, the decision of what and how much to produce and the decision of what and how much to consume were the same decision. Today these decisions are made separately, but they are connected by markets.

The product market and the factor market connect producers and consumers. This is shown in a simplified way by the circular flow diagram in Figure 0-1. The diagram is simplified (1) by assuming that business enterprises are the only producers in the economy and that households are the only consumers, (2) by assuming that only finished products are sold in the product market, and (3) by assuming that households are the sole owners of resources. In the *product market* businesses sell their output to households. In the *factor market* businesses buy the inputs which they combine to produce their output. These inputs are the services rendered by the *factors of production,* which are traditionally classified as *land, labor,* or *capital.* The market for steelworkers in Johnstown, Pennsylvania, and the market to rent farm land in Royal, Iowa, are factor markets. Producers acquire the services of these factors of production, transform them into goods and services, and sell the goods and services in product markets. The markets for bread and for haircuts are product markets.

The market mechanism binds the interdependent parts of the economy together. Each sale in the product market yields revenue which is distributed as income to the owners of the factors of production. Each dollar of income received in the factor market corresponds to a dollar spent in the product market.

The market mechanism registers the prices at which goods and services are bought and sold. In the product market business enterprises supply the output which consumers demand, and in the factor market the owners of the factors of production supply the inputs which enterprises demand. In both markets, supply and demand determine prices. At the same time these prices serve as indices of scarcity to buyers and sellers and help allocate the resources of the economy. The high price of diamonds reflects their scarcity and the low price of water indicates its abundance. Prices, or relative prices, determine whether our businessman will buy his computer and whether our restaurant customer will buy his hot dog. They influence how profitable motorcycle production will be, and how many will be produced.

But, how do supply and demand determine prices? And, what

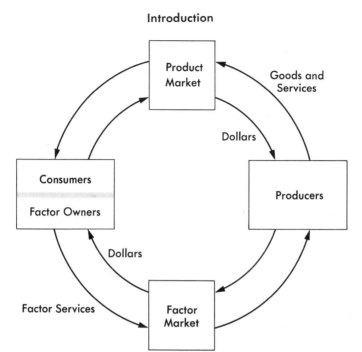

Figure 0-1.
The Circular Flow Diagram

determines supply and demand? These questions are answered in the chapters which follow.

The Plan of the Book

The arrangement of the remaining chapters can be explained in terms of the circular flow diagram. Suppose that the circle is cut and is stretched into a vertical line with the demand for products at the top and the supply of factors at the bottom. Conceptually, resources flow up the line from resource owners to producers to consumers. Chapter 1 discusses the elementary problems of supply and demand, and it applies to either the product market or the factor market. Chapters 2 through 7 are concerned with the flow from producers to consumers. They are concerned with the product market. Chapters 8 through 10 are concerned with the factor market.

Six chapters are spent on the product market, because this is

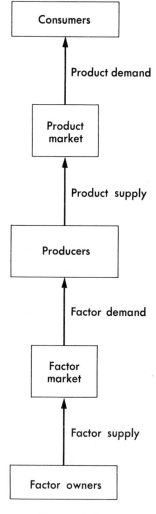

Figure 0-2.
The Plan of the Book

the core of price theory and because price theory is far more complicated than is suggested by Chapter 1—Elementary Supply and Demand. Chapter 2—Consumer Demand—develops some of the intricate problems associated with consumer demand. Chapter 3—Production and Costs—then skips to the supply side of the product market and discusses the laws of production and the costs of production which underlie the phenomenon of product supply.

The forces of supply and demand meet in the product market, where price is determined. Several chapters are needed to explain the determination of price, because there are several types of markets, each one different from the others. Markets are defined in terms of their structure, that is, in terms of their competitive environment. Chapter 4 deals with the *purely competitive* market, the market in which there are so many buyers and sellers that no one of them can influence the price. Chapter 5 discusses *pure monopoly*, where one firm has complete control over price or output. Between the extremes of pure competition and pure monopoly are monopolistically competitive and oligopolistic markets, both of which are characterized by a degree of competition and a degree of monopoly. Chapter 6 describes the *monopolistically competitive* market, where again there are many competitive buyers and sellers, but where each enterprise sells a slightly different variety of some product over which it has a small degree of monopoly control. In Chapter 7 *oligopoly* is treated. In such a market there are so few sellers that the actions of any one of them affects the others. They, therefore, recognize their mutual interdependence.

The last three chapters are concerned with the factor market, and they follow about the same order as the chapters on the product market. Chapter 8 develops the tools of supply and demand in the factor market. Households—the owners of resources—supply land, labor, and capital to enterprises. The demand for these resources by enterprises is determined by the productivity of the resources. Resource demand theory is called the *marginal productivity theory*, instead of price theory. Chapter 9 explains how supply and demand determine factor prices and income shares in competitive markets. Chapter 10 deals with the problems of monopoly in the factor market.

1

Elementary Supply and Demand

Many facts of our economic lives can be explained with the elementary tools of supply and demand. At any given moment the price of wheat or the price of AT & T stock can be explained in terms of supply and demand. Both the price of wheat and the price of AT & T stock are determined by the bargaining which balances the demand of buyers against the supply of sellers. Buyers bid one price, sellers ask another. The higgling of the market brings the two prices into equilibrium, so that contracts can be made and the exchange take place.

Competitive markets—markets in which there are so many buyers and sellers that no one of them can affect the equilibrium price—operate according to the impersonal laws of supply and demand. Where a degree of monopoly power exists, supply can be manipulated. Strictly speaking, the simple cases of supply and demand presented in this chapter do not explain monopoly prices. The law of supply describes the behavior of competitive sellers. The law of demand describes the behavior of buyers. Once these two laws are known, the price in competitive markets can be explained.

The Law of Demand

The *law of demand* states: the higher the price of a good, the smaller the quantity demanded; or, conversely, the lower the price, the greater the quantity demanded. The price of a good and the quantity demanded are inversely related. For example, people are ready to buy more oranges if the price of oranges happens to fall. The same people will tend to buy fewer oranges if the price rises.

Table 1-1 shows the prices which the people in a town are willing to pay for fresh oranges. Early in the season when only a few oranges are available, a few rich or extravagant people are willing to pay high prices for them. The first shipment of 5 dozen oranges may fetch a price as high as $.10 an orange or $1.20 a dozen. If the price were higher, a smaller quantity would be demanded. The price could go so high that no one would buy any. This would be the buyers' *reservation price*, above which they do not buy. As greater quantities become available, they can only be sold at lower prices. A second shipment of 15 dozen oranges can not be sold for $1.20 a dozen. If $1.20 were asked, many oranges would rot in the store. However, at $.90 a dozen people are willing to buy all 15 dozen, but no more. A third and still larger shipment of 30 dozen can be sold for exactly $.60 a dozen. If a store asked less than $.60 a dozen, people would demand more than the available 30 dozen. At $.45 a dozen they would demand 60 dozen oranges.

Table 1-1
The Demand for Oranges

	Dozens of Oranges Demanded	Price per Dozen
First Shipment	5	$1.20
Second Shipment	15	.90
Third Shipment	30	.60
Fourth Shipment	60	.45

The *demand schedule* which appears in Table 1-1 is presented graphically in Figure 1-1. In its graphical form it is called a *demand curve.* The demand curve slopes downward to the right because of the law of demand: the lower the price, the greater the quantity demanded.

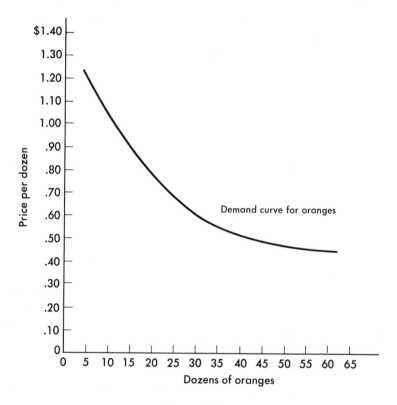

Figure 1-1.
The Demand for Oranges

A Note on Graphs. Graphs are used throughout this text. Frequently they are drawn from a table of numbers, just as Figure 1-1 is drawn from the numbers in Table 1-1. Whenever this is done, it is always assumed that the numbers in the table represent a set of points on a continuous line. For example, at $.60 a dozen, exactly 30 dozen oranges are demanded. At $.50 a dozen, approximately 40 dozen are assumed to be demanded, even though no numbers appear in Table 1-1 which correspond to this point. This should be kept in mind when studying the graphs.

The Law of Supply

The *law of supply* describes the behavior of sellers. It states that the higher the price, the greater the quantity supplied; or, the lower the price, the smaller the quantity supplied. Sellers are willing to supply larger quantities at high prices than at low prices. Every supplier has a price below which he will not sell. This is his *reservation price.* If price falls too low, he will hold his supply off the market and wait for the price to go up. This reservation price varies from seller to seller. As the price rises, more and more sellers become willing to supply a part or all of their goods. If price rises high enough, a point will come when every supplier will prefer to sell rather than hold his goods.

Table 1-2 presents a *supply schedule* for oranges. At $.25 a dozen no oranges will be supplied. There is not a single grocer who will sell at so low a price. They all prefer to wait for higher prices. At $.45 a dozen some grocers are willing to sell, so that 20 dozen oranges become available. As the price of oranges rises, greater quantities are supplied. More and more grocers become willing to sell more and more of their inventories. At $.60 a dozen, they supply 30 dozen; and at $.90 a dozen, they supply 36 dozen. Finally, at $1.20 a dozen, 40 dozen oranges are supplied. At so high a price all the grocers in town will sell all the oranges they have. At

Table 1-2
The Supply of Oranges

Dozens of Oranges Supplied	Price per Dozen
0	$ .25
20	.45
30	.60
36	.90
40	1.20
40	1.30

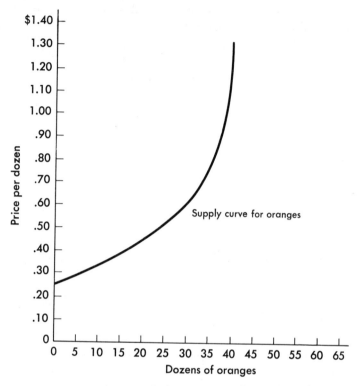

Figure 1-2.
The Supply of Oranges

$1.30 a dozen the same 40 dozen are supplied, for no greater quantity is immediately available. Table 1-2 is graphed in Figure 1-2.

The Equilibrium Price

The market forces of supply and demand determine the *equilibrium price.* The equilibrium price equates the quantity supplied and the quantity demanded. It balances the wants of buyers against the reservation prices of sellers. If price temporarily deviates from the equilibrium level, the competition of buyers and sellers tends to force it back toward the equilibrium level.

The determination of the equilibrium price of oranges is illustrated in Figure 1-3, which superimposes the supply curve from Figure 1-2 on the demand curve from Figure 1-1. The supply and demand curves intersect at a price of $.60 a dozen, where the quantity supplied equals the quantity demanded. Thus, by definition $.60 per dozen is the equilibrium price.

How is this equilibrium price established? Suppose the price is not at the equilibrium level. Suppose, for example, the price is

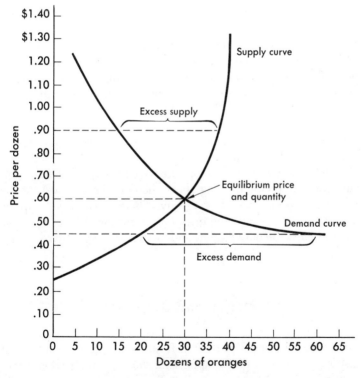

Figure 1-3.
The Equilibrium of the Supply and Demand for Oranges

temporarily at $.90 per dozen. At $.90 per dozen sellers supply 36 dozen, but buyers demand only 15 dozen. Supply exceeds demand. There is an *excess supply* at that price. An excess supply can exist only temporarily, because some grocers will not be able to sell their oranges at that price while they are willing to sell for less. They, therefore, will ask for less, and the market price will be forced down. At the lower price buyers purchase a larger quantity, thus reducing the excess supply. As long as there is an excess supply, the price will continue to fall toward the equilibrium level.

If the market price is below the equilibrium level, there is an *excess demand*. At $.45 per dozen buyers demand 60 dozen, while suppliers are willing to sell only 20 dozen. Who gets the 20 dozen? Anyone who pays more than the market price will certainly get what he wants; and, since there is an excess of buyers willing to pay more than $.45 per dozen, the price is bid up. The market price tends to move toward the equilibrium price.

The equilibrium adjustment is made in different ways in different markets. At an ordinary auction one item or lot is sold at a time. Supply is fixed. The auctioneer starts the bidding below the equilibrium price, so there is an excess demand, i.e., at the starting price more than one person is willing to buy the item. One person and then another bids the price up. As the price rises above what they are willing to pay, people drop out. The last bidder is the highest bidder, and he gets what has been offered for sale.

A dutch auction works the opposite way. Supply is still fixed, but the auctioneer starts the bidding above the equilibrium level. At the starting price no one is willing to buy. There is an excess supply. The auctioneer must lower the price until someone bids. In this case the first bidder is the only bidder, and he makes the purchase.

Shortages and Surpluses

When the market price is prevented from moving to its equilibrium level, shortages and surpluses appear. A *shortage* exists when there is an excess demand for a good. People want to buy more than is available at existing prices. A *surplus* exists when there is an excess supply. More is available for sale than people are willing to buy at existing prices. When existing prices move to their equilibrium, shortages and surpluses disappear.

For example, shortages in consumer goods occurred during World War II. The needs of the war created an excess demand for goods in general, and the tendency was for prices to rise. However, the government did not want prices to rise because that would inflict a great hardship on many people who had fixed incomes. To solve this problem, the government set legal limits, or ceilings, on the prices of many goods, making it a crime to sell above them.

Price ceilings proved to be only a partial solution. The fact remained that people demanded more goods than were supplied at these legal prices. This created a second issue. Who would get the available supplies? The families of soldiers? Munitions workers? First come, first serve? This secondary problem was solved by issuing ration coupons on many goods, particularly on necessities. Every household was given so many coupons to buy gasoline, so many to buy shoes, so many to buy meat, and so on. In other words, since the government did not want the market to allocate goods to the highest bidder, it had to devise another way of distributing the limited supplies.

To take another example, the newspapers often write about the problem of farm surpluses. These surpluses exist simply because the government has set farm prices above their equilibrium level in order to give farmers more income. However, it is not enough for the government to decree that farm prices shall be higher. To maintain these prices, the government must do something about the surplus which it has created. It must either buy up the surplus or restrict production. In fact, it has done both.

Figure 1-4 shows why shortages and surpluses exist. The market is in equilibrium at P_1, where the quantity supplied equals the quantity demanded. On the one hand, if the government sets price below the equilibrium level, say at P_2, a shortage occurs. People want to buy more than is supplied. On the other hand, if the government sets a price above the equilibrium level, a surplus appears. More is supplied than people want to buy. Left to itself, the market will tend to eliminate shortages and surpluses by pushing prices up or down. Those who are willing to pay the most get what they want, and those who sell for the least make the sales.

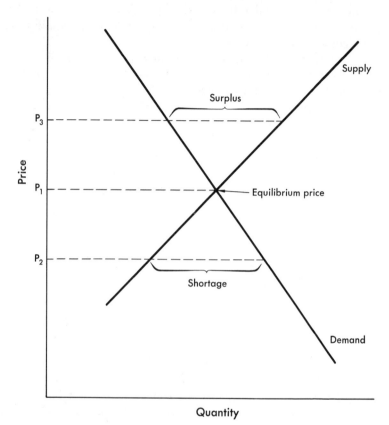

Figure 1-4.
Shortages and Surpluses

Shifts versus Movements

The equilibrium price is not the same forever. It changes from time to time in all markets, as the underlying forces of supply and demand change. On the New York Stock Exchange, the price of AT & T stock may move toward one equilibrium level in the morning and then move toward another in the afternoon, as buyers

and sellers hold first one view and then another. If sellers change
their minds, the supply curve will shift; and, if buyers change their
minds, the demand curve will shift.

The distinction between a *shift* in a supply or demand curve
and a *movement along* a given curve is shown in Figure 1-5. Start
with the Supply Curve and Demand Curve I. The equilibrium price
is $60 and the equilibrium quantity is 70,000 shares. Now, if buyers
change their minds and want to buy more at all prices, the demand
curve shifts from Demand Curve I to Demand Curve II. At the
old price ($60) a greater quantity is now demanded (100,000 shares)
than is supplied (70,000 shares). Prices are therefore bid up toward

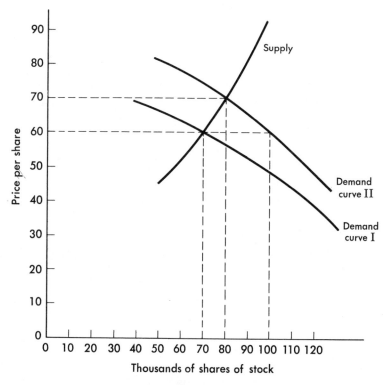

Figure 1-5.
A Shift in the Demand for AT & T Stock

the new equilibrium ($70). At the new equilibrium position a greater quantity is supplied (80,000 shares) than was supplied before (70,000 shares). In other words, there has been a *movement along* the supply curve due to a *shift* in demand.

When both the demand curve and the supply curve shift, a change in price cannot be attributed to either buyers or sellers, but must be attributed to both. Price changes in the stock market often are caused by shifts in both curves at the same time, and the influence of the one cannot always be separated from that of the other. However, the distinction between a bull market and a bear market is a distinction between a shift in a supply curve and a shift in a demand curve. In a *bull market,* prices rise and the volume of trading rises—the demand curve shifts up. In a *bear market,* prices fall and the volume of trading rises—the supply curve shifts down.

When demand shifts and supply is unchanged, prices move along the supply curve. An upward shift in demand increases price and quantity. A downward shift in demand decreases prices and quantity. When supply shifts and demand is unchanged, prices move along the demand curve. When supply shifts down, the quantity sold rises while the price falls. When supply is restricted and shifts up, prices rise as the quantity sold falls.

2

Consumer Demand

Consumer demand depends upon a great variety of things, both economic and noneconomic. On the economic side, the demand for a good depends upon three critical variables: the price of the good, the price of related goods, and the income of consumers. When one of these variables changes, the quantity of the good which people tend to buy changes. In addition, two other economic variables effect the demand for a good: advertising and differences in product quality.[1]

On the noneconomic side, consumer demand depends upon the behavioral and environmental forces which shape consumer preferences or tastes. These preferences are affected by the physical setting in which the individual finds himself. Individual desires also are molded by the social milieu in which he finds himself. Finally, demand is influenced by the exposure of the individual to new and different products. As the song goes, "How you gonna keep them down on the farm, after they've seen Paree?"

Economists focus their attention on the economic forces which determine demand and leave the noneconomic forces to social psychologists, advertising agencies, and others. The following sections of this chapter explain the relationship between consumer

[1] Advertising and product differentiation are discussed in Chapter 6.

demand for a good and the three critical variables of price, other prices, and income.

The Rationale Behind Demand

The theory of consumer demand has a long history and an extensive literature. Today, two theories are used to explain consumer demand. The first is called the *marginal utility theory,* and it is presented in the section which follows. The second is called *indifference curve analysis,* and it appears in an appendix to this chapter. The two theories are closely related. One can be translated into the other with slight modification.

The marginal utility theory was developed independently in the 1870's by three economists: Carl Menger, W. S. Jevons, and Leon Walras.[2] All three men were dissatisfied with the received theory of value. The older theory proposed that the price of a product was determined by its cost of production. The older theory offered a rough explanation of the price of many products, but it did not explain all prices. It did not, for example, explain the price of an art masterpiece whose modern price bears no relation to the original cost of the artist's labors. Indeed, it did not even explain the market price of many common farm products, because their prices typically change every day, sometimes by large amounts, while their cost of production only changes from year to year.

The marginal utility theory proposes that the price which people are willing to pay for different products is a *subjective* matter. Each consumer's likes, wants, and requirements determine the prices he is willing to pay for different products. Each consumer is assumed to spend his income in such a way that he maximizes his satisfaction. If one man likes wine, women, and song, he will spend his money on merriment. If a second man likes medieval manuscripts, Bach fugues, and Moorish castles, he will spend his money on such elegance. If a third man is a miser, he will not spend his money at all. Given his limited income and given his particular

[2] Carl Menger, *Principles of Economics* (New York: Free Press, 1950), originally published in 1871; W. S. Jevons, *The Theory of Political Economy* (New York: Kelley and Millman, 1957), originally published in 1871; and Leon Walras *Elements of Pure Economics* (Homewood, Ill.: Richard D. Irwin, 1954), originally published in 1874.

preferences, each man is assumed to maximize his material well-being, or what means the same thing, his total utility.

Wants are satiable. When a person buys more and more of a product, each additional unit adds less to his satisfaction than the one before. Each additional unit is of less use or utility to him. Technically speaking, the consumption of products is subject to the *principle of diminishing marginal utility. As a person consumes additional units of a product, the additional or marginal utility which the additional units yield diminishes.* For example, the utility that a person derives from a first pair of shoes is quite large. Without shoes his feet get cut, cold, and wet; and he is not accepted socially. A second pair of shoes is of use to him and it increases his total utility, but it adds less to his total utility than the first pair. A third pair of shoes adds still less to his total utility. The marginal utility which he derives from each additional pair of shoes diminishes.

While the wants of consumers are satiable, consumers want more than their incomes can buy. They must *choose* among all the various products they can buy. If they are rational, in the economic sense, they will choose that combination of products which maximizes their total utility. If a consumer has to choose between more hamburgers and more hot dogs, he will choose the one which adds the most to his total utility. He will be sure that the last dollar he spends on each product gives him the largest possible marginal utility. If the marginal utility he receives from his last dollar's worth of hamburgers exceeds the marginal utility he receives from his last dollar's worth of hot dogs, he will increase his total utility by purchasing more hamburgers and fewer hot dogs. As he purchases more hamburgers, their marginal utility diminishes; and, as he purchases fewer hot dogs, their marginal utility rises. When the marginal utility is equal for the last dollar he spends on every good, he can not increase his total utility by reallocating his spending. In other words, *total utility is at its maximum, when the price of each good—the last dollar spent on each good—yields proportionally the same marginal utility.* This is the *equal marginal principle,* and it is represented by the following expression:

$$\frac{\text{Marginal Utility of Hamburgers}}{\text{Price of Hamburgers}} = \frac{\text{Marginal Utility of Hot Dogs}}{\text{Price of Hot Dogs}} = \cdots$$

The equal marginal principle shows what combination of products maximizes consumer well-being—given consumer preferences, consumer income, and prices. If any of these givens change, the quantities demanded change. The quantity demanded of any product depends upon consumer preferences and the three critical economic variables: consumer income, the price of the product, and the prices of other products.

First, when consumer preferences change, the marginal utility of some products rises relative to the marginal utility of other products. The rational consumer changes accordingly the quantities which he demands. He buys more of those goods whose marginal utility has risen (relative to the marginal utility of other goods) and less of those goods whose marginal utility has fallen (relative to the marginal utility of other goods). As he buys more of some goods, their marginal utility falls; and, as he buys less of other goods, their marginal utility rises. He maximizes his total utility when the last dollar spent of each good yields the same marginal utility. If he receives more utility from the last dollar spent on one good than another, he will increase his total utility by buying more of the first good and less of the second. By buying in this way, he substitutes a larger for a smaller utility.

Second, when consumer income changes, the effective demand of the consumer changes. An *effective demand* is a want backed by purchasing power. For most goods, the quantity demanded will rise as income rises. Generally, people want more food, more clothing, and more shelter as their incomes rise; but they also want better qualities of food, clothing, and shelter. For this reason, the quantity of inferior quality goods which they demand may fall as their incomes rise, or rise as their incomes fall. Such goods are called *inferior goods*. As income rises, people want more beefsteak, not more potatoes. Therefore, the demand curve for potatoes may shift down while the demand curve for beefsteak shifts up.

Third, when the price of a good falls, the quantity demanded generally rises. This is the Law of Demand: the lower the price, the greater the quantity demanded; the higher the price, the smaller the quantity demanded. The law of demand holds true because consumers apply the equal marginal principle. When the price of a good suddenly falls relative to other prices, the last dollar spent on it will temporarily yield more utility than the last dollar spent on other goods. Since, at the lower price, more of the good can be purchased for one dollar than before, the marginal utility derived from the last dollar spent on the good must be greater than before. Consumers will, therefore, increase their total utility by purchasing more of the lower priced good and less of other goods. The tendency to substitute the lower priced good for other goods is known as the *substitution effect*.

A fall in the price of one good may produce an *income effect* in addition to a substitution effect. This idea was elaborated by J. R. Hicks in his book, *Value and Capital*.[3] When the price of a good falls, consumers are better off. In effect, they have more income. In the case of most goods, consumers will buy a larger quantity when they have a larger income. The effect on income produced by a fall in prices will, in most cases, reinforce the substitution effect: the lower the price, the greater the quantity demanded. In the case of inferior goods, however, the income effect leads consumers to buy smaller quantities as the price falls.

The law of demand is, therefore, generally true, but it is not universally true. The quantity demanded of some goods is greater at high prices than at low prices. This is true of a *Giffen good*.[4] A Giffen good is usually a necessity, like rice in Asia, which accounts for a large part of the expenditure of the poor. When the price of rice goes up, the poor have so little income left over they can no longer supplement their diets with more expensive foods and must buy more rice just to stay alive. In other words, the effect of the rise in the price of rice is to reduce incomes; and, since rice is an

[3] J. R. Hicks, *Value and Capital*, (Oxford: Clarendon Press, 1939), pp. 11–52. The addition of the income effect to the substitution effect permits the marginal utility theory to be presented in terms of the indifference curves. A demonstration of this, however, is beyond the scope of this book.

[4] The Giffen good exception to the law of demand would be excluded if we were to accept Milton Friedman's definition of the demand curve. See Milton Friedman, "The Marshallian Demand Curve," *Journal of Political Economy* (1949), pp. 463–95. He assumes that consumers have a constant real income (i.e., what income will buy in goods and services.) If real income is constant, then the effect of price changes on income must be ignored; and the Giffen good must be thrown out as an exception to the law of demand. Similarly, in the case of the Veblenesque good, it can be argued that consumer preferences ought to be defined so that they are independent of price changes. Under this definition, Veblenesque goods would have to be ruled out as an exception to the law of demand, since Veblenesque goods are preferred because they are high-priced.

inferior good, more is purchased as income falls. The law of demand does not apply to Giffen goods. It also does not apply to *Veblenesque goods* (named after the economist, Thorstein Veblen). Veblenesque goods are bought to enhance the prestige of the owner. High-priced whiskies are often served to reflect the taste and excellence of the host. If their prices were to fall to the common level, less might be bought.

Fourth, the quantity demanded of a particular good may rise or fall when the price of another good changes. If the quantity demanded of one good *rises* as the price of some other goods *rises,* the two goods are *substitutes.* As the price of the second good rises, people buy less of it and more of the first good. They substitute one for the other. For example, if the price of Danish rolls rises, one might expect people to switch to donuts. The demand curve for donuts would therefore shift to the right.

If the quantity demanded of a particular good *falls* as the price of some other good *rises,* the two goods are *complements.* Complements are used together. As the price of one rises, people tend to give up both. For example, if coffee and donuts are frequently consumed together, a rise in the price of coffee might lead people to buy fewer donuts as well as less coffee. The demand curve for donuts would shift to the left.

The law of demand assumes that "nothing else changes." It assumes that the prices of other goods and consumer incomes, as well as consumer preferences, do not change. When these things change, as they are constantly doing, the demand curve shifts, that is, a different quantity will be purchased at the same price. It is usual to assume that demand curves do not shift; or, if they shift, they shift once and for all. This simplification, which is maintained throughout this book, permits a detailed analysis of how enterprises, the owners of the factors of production, and markets adjust to known demand conditions.

The Elasticity of Demand

The *elasticity of demand* measures the responsiveness of the quantity demanded of a good to changes in its price, to changes in the price of other goods, and to changes in consumer income. Accordingly, there are three varieties of demand elasticity: price elasticity, cross elasticity, and income elasticity—one for each of the three critical variables. The concept of elasticity can be applied to supply as well as to demand; and it is an indispensable tool for businessmen, government officials, or anyone who is interested in analyzing the behavior of markets.

Price elasticity

The *price elasticity* of a good measures the responsiveness of the quantity demanded to changes in its price. This is also called direct elasticity. The businessman who is considering a change in the price of his product wants to know what will happen to his sales volume. The Model T Ford was a success because the demand for cars was very great at low prices. The increase in sales which resulted from marketing the low-priced Ford more than compensated for the fact that each car was sold at a lower price. On the other hand, when there is a bumper wheat crop, wheat prices tend to fall and to reduce farm receipts. The quantity of wheat demanded is relatively insensitive to price changes.

The price elasticity of a good is measured by the percentage change in the quantity demanded divided by the percentage change in price. When the quantity demanded changes by a larger percentage than the change in price, the demand curve is said to be *elastic.* For example, the demand for Model T's would be elastic if the number of cars sold rose 400% when prices were cut 50%. Such a hypothetical demand curve is graphed in Figure 2-1. A cut in price from $1,000 to $500 leads to an increase in the quantity sold from 100,000 to 400,000 cars per year. Because quantity rises more than in proportion to the fall in price, sales revenue increases from $100 million (= $1,000 × 100,000) to $200 million (= $500 × 400,000).

When the quantity demanded changes by a smaller percentage than the change in price, the demand curve is said to be *inelastic.* For example, if a 50% cut in the price of wheat leads to only a 10% increase in the quantity sold, the demand for wheat is inelastic. People are relatively insensitive to changes in wheat prices. In Figure 2-2, the price of wheat is shown to fall from $2.00 to $1.00,

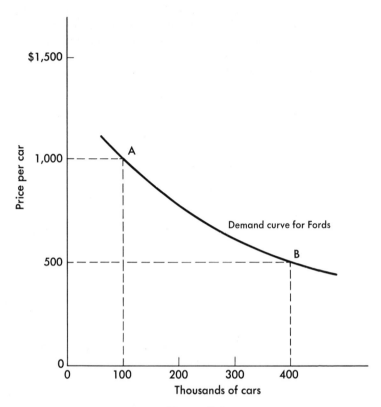

Figure 2-1.
The Demand for Model T Fords

but the quantity sold increases from only 1.0 to 1.1 million bushels. As a result, farmers suffer a loss in revenue from $2.0 million (= $2 × 1 million bushels) to $1.1 million (= $1 × 1.1 million bushels).

Finally, there are three special cases of price elasticity. (1) a horizontal demand curve is said to be *perfectly elastic*. When the demand curve facing the individual businessman is perfectly elastic, he can sell all he can produce without affecting the price level. This is the case of the individual businessman in a purely competitive market. (2) A vertical demand curve is said to be *perfectly inelastic*.

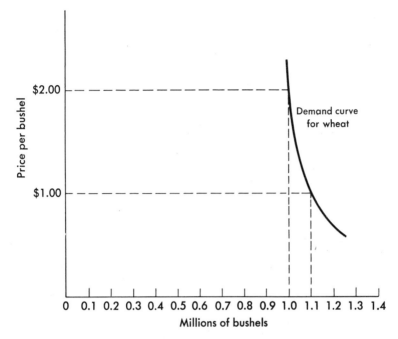

Figure 2-2.
The Demand for Wheat

(3) A demand curve is said to be *unitarily elastic* when the percentage change in quantity equals the percentage change in price. Here, sales revenue does not change as price falls. It remains constant, because the addition to revenue resulting from the increase in the quantity sold just offsets the fall in price. These special cases are graphed in Figure 2-3.

The price elasticity of demand can be expressed as a number. This number, the *coefficient of elasticity*, can be calculated from the following formula, the formula for *arc elasticity*.

$$\text{Elasticity coefficient} = \frac{\dfrac{Q_a - Q_b}{Q_a + Q_b}}{\dfrac{P_a - P_b}{P_a + P_b}}$$

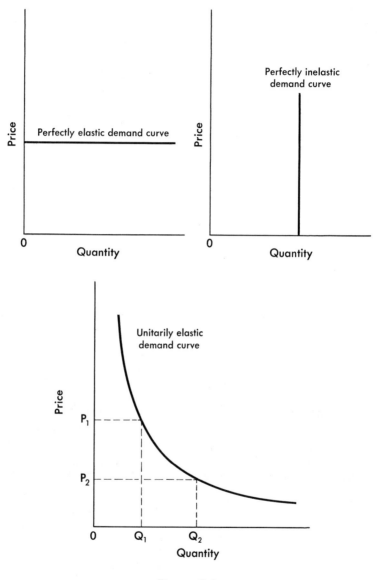

Figure 2-3.
Three Special Cases of Demand Elasticity

where subscripts "a" and "b" refer to points A and B in Figure 2-1, respectively. Arc elasticity is so named because it measures elasticity along a segment or arc of a demand curve. Arc elasticity is distinguished from point elasticity, the elasticity at a point (e.g., A) on a demand curve.

While the coefficient of the price elasticity of demand is generally negative, it is usually expressed as a positive number. When price elasticity is greater than one, the demand curve is relatively elastic. The demand curve for the Model T Ford in Figure 2-1 is elastic. It has a coefficient of 1.8. That is,

$$\frac{100-400}{100+400} \div \frac{1000-500}{1000+500} = \frac{-300}{500} \times \frac{1500}{500} = -\frac{9}{5}.$$

Or, ignoring the minus sign, 1.8. When the coefficient of elasticity is less than one, the demand curve is relatively inelastic. This is the case of the demand for wheat. The coefficient for wheat is 0.14. That is,

$$\frac{1.0-1.1}{1.0+1.1} \div \frac{2-1}{2+1} = \frac{-.1}{2.1} \times \frac{3}{1} = -\frac{1}{7}.$$

Or, ignoring the minus sign, 0.14. A unitarily elastic demand curve has a coefficient of one or unity.

Cross elasticity

Cross elasticity measures the responsiveness of the quantity demanded of one good to changes in the price of another good. It is concerned with two different goods. In the case of substitutes, the quantity demanded of one good goes up, when the price of the other good goes up. If the price of Danish rolls rises, the quantity of donuts sold rises, as buyers switch to donuts. The change in relative prices changes the quantities demanded. In the case of complements, the quantity demanded of one good goes up, when the price of the other good goes down. For example, if the price of jam falls, bread sales may rise; for, in order to take advantage of the lower price of jam, people buy more bread.

The arc elasticity formula can be used to calculate cross elasticities by having the "Q's" refer to one good and the "P's" to another. Goods which are unrelated have cross elasticity coefficients near zero. Close substitutes have large positive coefficients, and close complements have large negative cross elasticity coefficients.

Income elasticity

Finally, income elasticity relates the responsiveness of the quantity demanded of a good to changes in income. The demand curve for a good generally shifts to the right when the incomes of consumers rise. During the boom phase of a business cycle more of most goods are purchased. However, inferior goods suffer a fall in demand as income rises. For example, the demand for dry milk may fall as incomes rise because with higher incomes, people will buy whole milk instead. The income elasticity of ordinary goods is positive; the income elasticity of inferior goods is negative.

Total Revenue and Elasticity

The demand curve shows how much consumers are willing to pay for various quantities of a good; it also shows how much revenue business enterprises will receive. The demand curve itself is an *average revenue* schedule. It shows the price per unit at which each quantity sells. *Total revenue* is simply price times quantity. Graphically, it is the area of a rectangle inscribed by the demand curve.

In Figure 2-4, when the price is $5, total revenue equals $10, because two units are demanded at that price ($10 = $5 × 2). When the price is $4, total revenue is $12. Notice that total revenue rises as price falls. It rises from $10 to $12. This means that, within the range of $4 to $5, the demand curve is elastic. The percentage rise in quantity exceeds the percentage fall in price. At a price of $2, total revenue is $10 ($2 × 5 = $10). And, at $1, the total revenue is $6. Thus, within the range of $1 to $2, the demand curve is inelastic. The percentage fall in price exceeds the percentage rise in quantity, so that a fall in price reduces total revenue.

In Table 2-1, total revenue is calculated for the demand curve in Figure 2-4. Total revenue rises from zero at $7 where nothing is bought to $12 at a price of $4 or $3 and then falls to zero again as

Table 2-1
Total Revenue and Elasticity

Price	×	Quantity	=	Total Revenue	Marginal Revenue	Elasticity
7		0		0		
6		1		6	6	
5		2		10	4	Relatively elastic
4		3		12	2	
3.50		3.50		12.25	0	Unitarily elastic
3		4		12		
2		5		10	−2	Relatively inelastic
1		6		6	−4	
0		7		0	−6	

price falls to zero. Since total revenue rises when price falls from $7 to $4 (or, to $3.50, to be exact), the demand curve is elastic at all prices above $4. Similarly, since total revenue falls when price

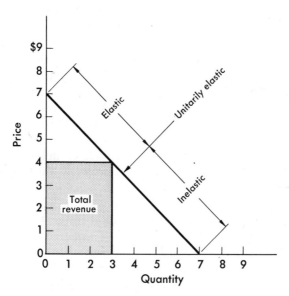

Figure 2-4.
Demand and Elasticity

falls below $3 (below $3.50 to be exact), the demand curve is inelastic at all prices below $3. At exactly $3.50, total revenue is at its maximum and the area of the rectangle under the demand curve is at its maximum. At that point the demand curve is unitarily elastic, for as the price falls past that point, elasticity passes from being greater than one to being less than one. At that point elasticity must equal one.

Marginal Revenue

The *marginal* concept is of central importance in price theory. Price theory is sometimes described as marginalism. However, the marginal concept is not limited to economics. It has many academic and many everyday uses. For example, how can one tell whether the ocean tide is at its low, at its high, coming in, or going out? At a glance, one cannot tell provided he hasn't memorized the tide table. In time he can tell if he watches the water's edge or margin. When the tide is coming in, the edge or margin of the ocean rises; when it is going out, the margin falls. At low tide and at high tide there is temporarily no change. Just before high tide the margin is rising, just after the margin is falling. At high tide the marginal change is zero. At low tide, this sequence is reversed.

In a similar way the businessman cannot tell whether his revenues are at their maximum by looking at one total revenue figure. He must watch his marginal revenue. *Marginal revenue is defined as the change in total revenue associated with a change in the quantity sold.* If a reduction in his price (which necessarily increases the quantity sold) adds something to his revenue, then his total revenue was previously not at its maximum. His marginal revenue is positive. Similarly, if a reduction in his price subtracts something from his revenue, then his total revenue cannot be not at its maximum. His marginal revenue is negative. As long as his marginal revenue is positive, he can increase his total revenue by lowering his price; and, as long as his marginal revenue is negative, he can increase his total revenue by increasing his price (reducing the quantity sold).

Figure 2-5 shows the relationship between the demand curve,

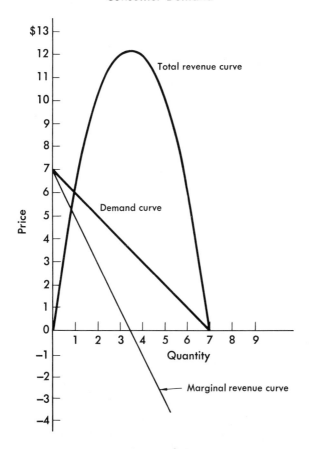

Figure 2-5.
Demand, Total Revenue, and Marginal Revenue

total revenue, and marginal revenue. Marginal revenue is calculated in Table 2-1 by subtracting the first total revenue from the second ($6 — $0 = $6), the second from the third ($10 — $6 = $4), and so on. As price falls from $7.00 to $3.50, total revenue rises and marginal revenue is positive. As price falls below $3.50, total revenue falls and marginal revenue is negative. Where marginal revenue is zero, total revenue is at its maximum.

It should be noticed that marginal revenue is positive where the demand curve is elastic, that marginal revenue is negative where the demand curve is inelastic, and that marginal revenue is zero where the demand curve is unitarily elastic. This is necessarily true because of the way the various concepts are defined.

The importance of the concept of elasticity and of its relation to revenue is illustrated by an example taken from Augustin Cournot's *The Mathematical Principles of the Theory of Wealth* (1838).[5] Consider the problem of a man who owns a mineral spring which has unique curative properties. Being the owner of the mineral spring, he can exclude others from using it. Being a man of affairs, he wants to make the most of it. Being a monopolist, he can sell at any price he pleases. Question: what price should he charge to gain the most revenue? Should he charge the highest possible price? No. If the demand for his mineral water is that shown in Figure 2-5, he will maximize his revenue by charging a price between $3.00 and $4.00 a unit, $3.50 to be exact. At that price the area of a rectangle under the demand curve is at a maximum. To put it another way, he will charge a price such that his marginal revenue is zero. Where his marginal revenue is still positive, he can add to his total revenue by lowering his price and selling more. If his marginal revenue is negative, he is taking away from the total. Where marginal revenue just equals zero, he maximizes his total revenue. All this assumes that he has no costs, or none worth mentioning, which is hardly common. Costs change the picture somewhat. They are examined in the next chapter.

[5] Augustin Cournot, *The Mathematical Principles of the Theory of Wealth* (Homewood, Ill., Richard D. Irwin, 1963), pp. 46–54; originally published in 1838.

Appendix to Chapter 2

The Theory of Consumer Demand: Indifference Curve Analysis

The theory of consumer demand offers an explanation of how the quantity demanded of a good is related to its price, to the price of other goods, and to the income of consumers. It assumes that the noneconomic factors which alter consumer preferences are constant and, therefore, that each consumer has a given set of preferences. Given his particular preferences, each consumer chooses those goods that maximize his satisfaction. He is limited by his income and by the prices which he must pay for various goods.

One way in which the theory of consumer demand can be presented is known as indifference curve analysis. An *indifference curve* shows the preferences of an individual consumer. It shows two goods in various combinations between which the individual consumer is indifferent. He would just as soon have one combination as another. Table 2-2 shows various combinations of hot dogs and hamburgers which satisfy some hypothetical consumer to the same extent. In the course of a week, he would be just as satisfied with 13 hot dogs and 1 hamburger as he would be with 1 hot dog and 10 hamburgers. Table 2-2 is graphed in Figure

Table 2-2
Consumer Indifference Between Hot Dogs and Hamburgers

Combination	Hot Dogs	Hamburgers
A	13	1
B	8	2
C	4	4
D	2	7
E	1	10

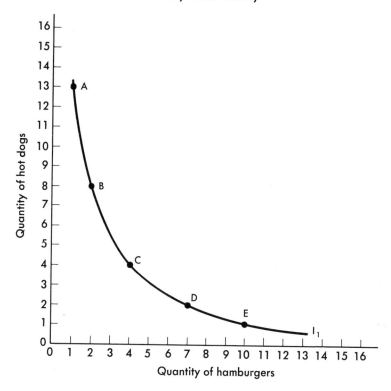

Figure 2-6.
A Consumer Indifference Curve

2-6. Each combination (A, B, C, D, and E) represents one point on the indifference curve. The indifference curve is labeled I_1.

The indifference curve in Figure 2-6 is curved in toward the origin of the graph. This reflects the high value which consumers place on variety. Consumers are rarely satisfied with great amounts of one good and none of others. They prefer an assortment of many. It takes increasing quantities of one good to induce them to give up each additional unit of another good. For example, when the consumer moves from point C to point B, he must gain 4 hot dogs to compensate him for the loss of 2 hamburgers; and when he moves from B to A, he must gain 5 hot dogs to compensate him for his loss of 1 hamburger if he is to remain indifferent.

While the individual consumer is indifferent between 4 hot dogs and 4 hamburgers, he would prefer more of both. He would prefer 6 and 6. However, this combination is not on indifference curve I_1. It appears in Figure 2-7 on indifference curve I_2, which shows combinations of larger quantities at every point and which gives the consumer a greater degree of satisfaction at every point than does indifference curve I_1. For each degree of satisfaction there is a separate indifference curve, each showing a combination of quantities between which the individual consumer is indifferent.

When several indifference curves are drawn on the same graph, as in Figure 2-7, the graph is called an indifference map, because it resembles the elevation contours on a map. Each elevation represents a

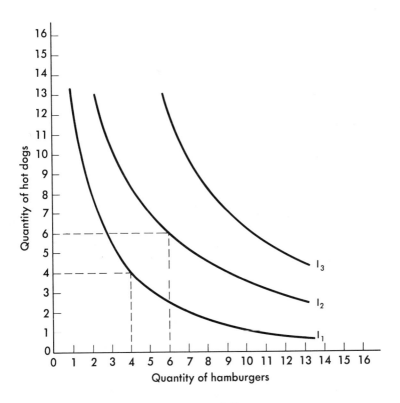

Figure 2-7.
An Indifference Map

different degree of satisfaction: the higher the elevation, the greater the degree of satisfaction.

Once the consumer's indifference map is known, it is possible to show the influence of prices and income on the quantities he demands. If the consumer in Figure 2-7 has an allowance of $3.00 a week and if both hot dogs and hamburgers cost $.25 a piece, he can buy a variety of combinations. He can buy 12 hot dogs and no hamburgers or 12 hamburgers and no hot dogs ($.25 × 12 = $3.00). He can buy 11 hot dogs and 1 hamburger, or 10 hot dogs and 2 hamburgers, or any other combination which adds up to $3.00. His income is limited to $3.00, and he can spend no more. The various combinations which he can spend are shown by the *budget line* in Figure 2-8.

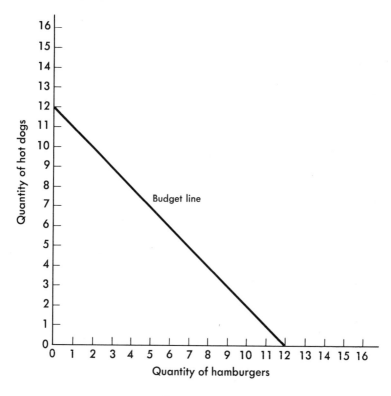

Figure 2-8.
A Budget Line

Which combination will he buy? To put the same question in graphical terms, how high up his indifference hill will his budget let him go? When the budget line of Figure 2-8 is superimposed on the indifference map of Figure 2-7 (see Figure 2-9), it can be seen that indifference curve I_2 is the highest curve that his budget line can reach. He will buy 6 hot dogs and 6 hamburgers, which is the combination corresponding to the point of tangency between indifference curve I_2 and his budget line. At that point, with that combination, he maximizes his satisfaction. If he bought any other combination, he would move to a lower level of satisfaction.

What happens when income changes? Suppose the allowance of our hypothetical consumer is increased to $4.00. Now he can buy 16 hot

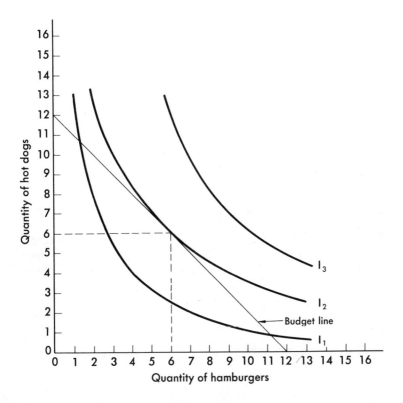

Figure 2-9.
Maximum Consumer Satisfaction

dogs or 16 hamburgers at $.25 apiece, or any other combination which adds up to $4.00. In Figure 2-10 his new budget line is to the right of and parallel to his old budget line. Therefore, the new line touches a higher indifference curve (I_3). When he now maximizes his satisfaction, he buys more hot dogs and more hamburgers, provided neither is an inferior good. If one were an inferior good, he would buy less of it as his income increased. In Figure 2-10 the shape of the indifference map shows that neither hot dogs nor hamburgers are considered to be inferior goods by this particular consumer. He buys more of both: 7 hot dogs and 9 hamburgers.

What happens when prices change? Suppose our consumer still has his $4.00 allowance, and suppose that the price of hamburgers rises to

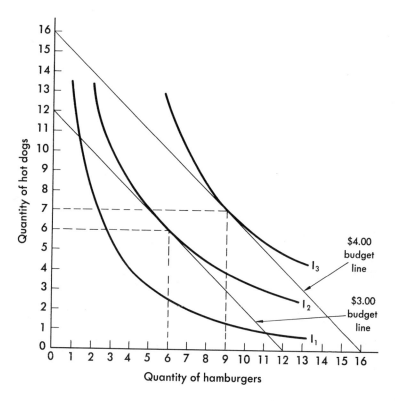

Figure 2-10.
An Increase in the Consumer Budget

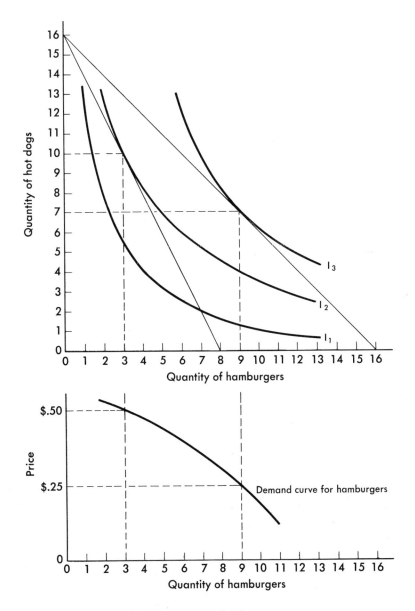

Figure 2-11.
The Demand Curve for Hamburgers Derived from an Indifference Map

43

$.50 each, while the price of hot dogs stays at $.25 each. He can still buy as many as 16 hot dogs if he buys no hamburgers, but he can only buy 8 hamburgers if he buys no hot dogs ($.50 × 8 = $4.00). His new budget line has a steeper slope than his first budget line, indicating that the price of hamburgers has risen relative to the price of hot dogs. See the top portion of Figure 2-11. The highest level of satisfaction he can now reach is where indifference curve I_2 is tangent to his new budget line, that is, where he buys 10 hot dogs and 3 hamburgers.

A demand curve can be derived from the indifference curves in Figure 2-11. When the price of hamburgers rises from $.25 to $.50, the individual consumer reduces the purchases of hamburgers from 9 to 3. In the lower portion of Figure 2-11, prices replace hot dogs on the vertical axis. At $.50 each, 3 hamburgers are demanded; at $.25 each, 9 hamburgers are demanded. The line which connects these two points is a demand curve, and it follows the law of demand: the lower the price, the greater the quantity demanded.

3

Production and Cost

In order to estimate its profit, a business enterprise must know its cost of production as well as the revenue from its sales. All business enterprises use the following basic equation to calculate profit: Total Revenue = Total Cost + Profit. If total cost exceeds total revenue, the enterprise has a loss, not a profit.

Cost and revenue reduce to prices and quantities. The cost of production depends upon two things: the prices of different kinds of inputs and the quantities of input used. For example, total labor cost equals the price of labor times the quantity of labor used $(P_1 \times Q_1)$. Similarly, total capital cost equals the price of capital times the quantity used $(P_c \times Q_c)$. Total revenue equals the price of each type of output multiplied by the quantity sold, e.g., $P_g \times Q_g + P_h \times Q_h$, where g and h are two different types of output sold by the enterprise. Now the basic equation can be rewritten in terms of prices and quantities:

$$P_g \times Q_g + P_h \times Q_h = P_1 \times Q_1 + P_c \times Q_c + \text{Profit}.$$

Technology relates one quantity to another. The following section on the laws of production describes the general technical relationships which an enterprise must know if it is to operate profitably. Profitability is not just a matter of technology. The business enterprise must also know the price or scarcity of various inputs and outputs. The section on costs is concerned with the most economical use of scarce inputs.

Laws of Production

Every enterprise has a *production function* which describes how various kinds of inputs can be combined to produce one or more products. This production function can be separated into four technical relationships. First, there is the technical connection between one input and one output, assuming that other inputs and outputs remain constant. This relationship follows the law of diminishing returns. Second, there is the relationship between different outputs which describes the production possibilities of a business with given resources. Third, there is the possibility of using different combinations of inputs to produce a given output. This involves the principle of factor substitution. Fourth, there is the variation in output which results from changing all inputs in the same proportion. This relationship traces the economies of large scale production. These four relationships may apply to a single plant, an industry, or an entire economy.

The law of diminishing returns

The law of diminishing returns states: *as additional units of a variable input are taken into production, output will increase, but eventually the additional output attributable to the additional input will diminish,* assuming at least one type of input is fixed and assuming technology does not change. A man working a fixed 5 acres of land can increase his output by using more inputs. He can get more and more corn if he uses more and more fertilizer, seed, water, and labor. However, as he adds more input to his fixed 5 acres, output eventually increases by smaller and smaller amounts, that is, output is subject to diminishing returns. If this were not true, it would be possible to increase the output of a small 5 acre farm until it supplied all the needs of the world by merely adding more labor, equipment, and supplies.

A numerical example of the law of diminishing returns is presented in Table 3-1, which uses some technical, though easily understood, language. *Total product* (corn) increases as successive

Table 3-1
The Law of Diminishing Returns

Variable Input Labor (man-days)	Fixed Input Land (acres)	Total Product Corn (bushels)	Average Product Corn (bushels)	Marginal Product Corn (bushels)
0	5	0	—	2
1	5	2	2	4
2	5	6	3	6
3	5	12	4	7
4	5	19	$4\frac{3}{4}$	6
5	5	25	5	5
6	5	30	5	4
7	5	34	$4\frac{6}{7}$	3
8	5	37	$4\frac{5}{8}$	2
9	5	39	$4\frac{3}{9}$	1
10	5	40	4	$\frac{1}{2}$
11	5	$40\frac{1}{2}$	$3\frac{15}{22}$	

units of the *variable input* (labor) are added to the *fixed input* (land). *Average product* is total product per worker—total output divided by the number of laborers. *Marginal product* is the change in total product corresponding to a change in the variable input. Marginal product is calculated in the following way:

$$\text{Marginal Product} = \frac{\text{Change in Total Product}}{\text{Change in Variable Input}}$$

When the first laborer is employed, the marginal product is 2. When the second laborer is added, the marginal product is 4. The output rises by 4 as the variable input rises by 1.

$$MP = \frac{6-2}{2-1} = 4$$

At first, as shown in Table 3-1, the marginal product increases. The total product increases at an increasing rate. The third laborer increases the total product by 6 bushels, and the fourth laborer adds 7 bushels to the total product. As more laborers are added, the total product will continue to rise, but, at a certain point, the marginal product will begin to diminish. When the fifth man is added, the total product rises from 19 to 25 bushels. The marginal product is 6. When the sixth man is added, the total product rises from 25 to 30 bushels, so that marginal product is 5. It is possible that, if too many laborers were added, they would get in each other's way and actually reduce total output, but businesses are unlikely to reach that point.

Table 3-1 is graphed in Figure 3-1. The output of corn appears on the vertical axis, and the input of labor appears on the horizontal axis. Total product, average product, and marginal product are drawn as continuous lines. They are drawn as if small fractions had been inserted between the numbers shown in Table 3-1. The marginal product data corresponds to the midpoints between the variable input data. It is the change in total product when one laborer is added or subtracted.[1]

When the first few laborers are employed, total product increases at an increasing rate. This might be due to the possibility of using more specialized work assignments as the labor force expands. One man makes the furrow, the second man drops in the seed, the third man covers it—all in less time than it would take if each man did all three operations. Eventually, marginal product turns down. In Figure 3-1 where the lines are continuous, marginal product turns down after 3½ laborers are employed, or after 3 men are employed for a whole day and one man is employed for half a day. Table 3-1 does not show half days of labor; but, if it did, it would show that marginal product begins to diminish from 3½ man-days of labor. Finally, total product reaches its peak at 40½ bushels, after which it would decline if more laborers were employed.[2]

The law of diminishing returns, like other technical relation-

[1] Marginal product is the *change* in total product associated with a *change* in the variable input. For example, total product rises 7 bushels when the 4th laborer is added. Total product falls 7 bushels when the 4th laborer is subtracted and only 3 laborers remain. Marginal product is 7 between the point that 3 laborers and the point that 4 laborers are employed. For convenience, it is assumed to equal 7 at the midpoint—3½ man-days. Where lines are continuous, each point on the marginal product curve corresponds to an infinitesimally small change in total product.

[2] The area of diminishing returns is defined as that range of output between the point that average product is a maximum and the point that total product is a maximum.

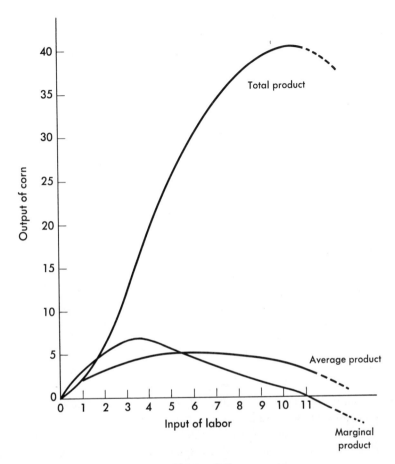

Figure 3-1.
The Law of Diminishing Returns

ships, expresses a purely physical relationship. It does not show the most profitable level of operation, and it does not show the most efficient level of operation. In order to know what is profitable and what is efficient, the relative prices (the relative scarcities) of inputs and outputs must be known. It is possible to get more than 200 bushels of corn from an acre of land, if enough labor, fertilizer, and supplies are used to cultivate it. However, such intensive farming would be unprofitable if the cost exceeded the revenue; it

would be inefficient if the application of the same resources elsewhere yielded a greater output.

The law of diminishing returns has long been recognized. T.
R. Malthus used it in his essay *On Population* (1798),[3] in which he
developed the theory that population always tends to surpass the
production of food and that this population pressure tends to im-
poverish mankind. Population increases at a geometric rate, while
food production increases at an arithmetic rate. Food production
cannot be increased at the same rate that population increases
because the land area suitable for cultivation is limited. Whenever
food production rises temporarily above a subsistence level, the
higher standard of living encourages reproduction and permits the
survival of a larger population. The growth of population forces
the standard of living down again as more people must live off the
same area of land. This theory has won wide acceptance. It is one
of the chief postulates of Charles Darwin's *The Origin of Species*
(1859); [4] and it is a dilemma facing many underdeveloped countries.

One important thing that Malthus overlooked was the great
increases in production which could come with technological
progress. In the economically advanced countries, the development
of scientific agriculture—crop rotation, selective breeding, and
fertilization—and the mechanization of agriculture—tractors, combines, and corn pickers—has increased food output more rapidly
than population. The law of diminishing returns applies when
technology does not change and when at least one input (such as
land) cannot be increased.

A change in technology would be represented as an upward
shift in the total product and marginal product curves of Figure
3-1. Throughout this book the same assumption about shifts in
product curves will be made as was made about shifts in demand
curves. If they shift, they shift once and for all.

Production possibilities

A business firm or a national economy which has a given
amount of resources with which to work has a limit to its production

[3] T. R. Malthus, *On Population* (New York: Random House, 1960), originally
published in 1798.
[4] Charles Darwin, *The Origin of Species* (New York: New American Library,
1962), originally published in 1859.

possibilities. It cannot produce more of everything. In fact, when it is using all its resources, it cannot produce more of anything without sacrificing something else. As a matter of fact, equal reductions in the output of one product will only free enough resources to permit the output of a second product to increase at a diminishing rate.

A *production possibilities curve* shows the *maximum* quantity of one good that can be produced, given various levels of output of a second good. It is drawn concave to the origin of the graph because the substitution of one output for another is subject to a *diminishing rate of transformation. The output of one good will increase at a diminishing rate as the output of a second good is reduced by successive equal amounts,* provided a constant quantity of resources are employed and provided technology does not change. The output of either or both goods can fall short of the production possibilities curve, but the output of neither can exceed it. The curve shows the *frontier* of production possibilities.

The diminishing rate of transformation between two outputs is due to the law of diminishing returns. When a war ends, for example, resources are freed from the production of guns and can enter the production of butter. As more men, more equipment, and more supplies are combined with the limited amount of land suitable for dairy farming, the output of butter increases, but it increases at a diminishing rate. As a result, for each equal reduction in the production of guns, the output of butter rises at a diminishing rate.

When the United States entered World War II, it could increase munitions production without cutting back on total consumer goods output because the economy was operating well under its potential. In 1940, over 8 million men were unemployed, since the economy was still in the grip of the Great Depression. The rise in munitions production during the war eliminated unemployment. When the war ended, production remained near capacity, while demand shifted away from munitions to consumer goods. As Figure 3-2 shows, the first reductions in national defense expenditures permitted relatively large increases in personal consumption expenditures. By 1946, the continuing reduction in defense production yielded much smaller increases in consumer goods output. Thus, for the nation "guns and butter" were not perfect substitutes, but increasing quantities of the one had to be sacrificed in order to get equal increases in the other. The production possibilities curve shows the alternative goods and services which can be produced. Demand determines which of them are produced.

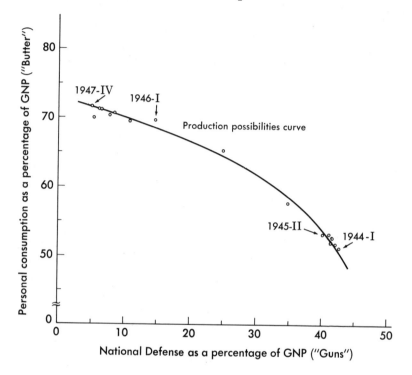

Figure 3-2.
Guns and Butter

Note: Line is fitted by hand. Personal Consumption and National Defense are in constant dollars (adjusted for price changes) and are expressed as percentages of GNP to eliminate the effect of changes in GNP. The change in the composition of GNP is graphed.

As an economy grows, its production possibilities curves shift out. However, price theory is not a theory of growth, but a theory of resource allocation with a given technology, given resources, and a known demand structure. It is possible to plot the production possibilities curve in Figure 3-2 because the time period was short —technology and resources could be treated as constants.

Factor substitution

The third law of production—the principle of factor substitution—involves the substitution of one input for another, and it is subject to a kind of diminishing returns like the first two laws. One factor of production can often be substituted for another, as aluminum for steel, for example, but factors of production are infrequently perfect substitutes. Steel is stronger, heavier, and a poorer conductor than aluminum. The principle of factor substitution states that, *as successive equal quantities of a first input are added to production, a second input can only be withdrawn at a diminishing rate if output is to remain constant.*

Aluminum can be substituted for steel in the production of automobiles. There are some functions that aluminum may perform better than steel. The heat conductivity of aluminum suits it for use in the engine block. There are other functions, e.g., the body work, that the two metals may perform equally well. Still other things are done better by steel, e.g., the making of gears and axles. As more aluminum is used to produce an automobile, the quantity of steel used can be reduced, but only at a diminishing rate. Of course, the most profitable combination cannot be calculated without knowing the prices at which all inputs can be purchased. The fall in the price of aluminum relative to the price of steel over the course of this century has induced metal fabricators of all kinds to substitute aluminum for steel.

Capital can be substituted for labor, as the businessman in the Introduction substituted a computer for bookkeepers in order to make out his payroll. He would probably keep some bookkeepers. If he had tried to replace them all with computers, he might have found himself spending more for the additional computers than he was saving on the bookkeepers. If this were the case, he would be experiencing a diminishing rate of factor substitution.

Returns to scale

Returns to scale describes what happens to the output of an enterprise when all inputs vary in proportion. Returns to scale describe what will happen to output when twice as much land, twice as much labor, and twice as much capital are brought into production. No doubt output will increase as the scale of the productive organization is increased, but will output increase by the same percentage as the increase in inputs?

No law of returns to scale exists because output per unit input may rise, fall, or remain the same as all inputs are increased in proportion. An enterprise may experience *increasing returns, constant returns,* or *decreasing returns* to scale as the size of its operations are increased. (1) Increasing returns to scale (economies of scale) occur in industries where large scale plants produce more output per unit input than small scale plants. Mass production industries, like the automobile industry, benefit from increasing returns. If an automobile company expects to compete in the national market, it must have a sizable factory. (2) Constant returns mean that large and small plants use the same proportion of inputs to outputs. (3) Decreasing returns to scale (diseconomies of scale) exist where small plants produce more output per unit input than large plants. Barber shops, automobile repair shops, and taverns are typically small and numerous, suggesting that such firms may suffer from diseconomies as their size increases.

Unlike the first three laws of production, there is no reason why returns to scale need eventually decrease in all industries. The forces which generate increasing and decreasing returns are unrelated. Two phenomena explain increasing returns. First, output per unit input may increase as the size of the plant is increased due to technical factors. For example, the efficiency of the chemical reaction in a blast furnace increases with the volume of the furnace. More pig iron is produced for each ton of ore, coke, or limestone. Thus, there are economies of scale in the operation of large blast furnaces. Second, economies of scale arise from the division of labor and the specialization of equipment. Increased specialization permits greater mastery of an operation, and with specialization, less time is lost moving from one operation to another.

Diseconomies of scale are usually explained by the limits to decision making. As an enterprise grows, the parts become more and more numerous, farther and farther apart, and more and more difficult to coordinate. This reduces productivity: output per unit input falls.

Costs

The businessman cannot decide how much of a good to supply without knowing how much it costs to produce. Cost calculations give financial meaning to the laws of production by putting prices on physical quantities. The total cost of production equals the price of various inputs multiplied by the quantities of inputs used. Output rises or falls and costs rise or fall as more or fewer inputs are used. When the businessman knows both his cost of production and the demand for his product, he can decide which level of output is the most profitable. In other words, he can decide how much to supply.

The *opportunity cost* principle is the most important cost concept that a business enterprise can use, and it is the most important cost concept in economics. The opportunity cost principle compares the cost of one alternative with the cost of another alternative; or, what amounts to the same thing, it compares the benefit derived from one action with the benefit derived from an alternative action. The opportunity cost of doing anything is the value of what could have been done instead. The real cost to a man of becoming a dishwasher is what he could have earned instead by becoming a mechanic, an electrician, or a bricklayer.

The principle of factor substitution is a technical matter that relates one input to another. The principle of opportunity cost determines what combination of inputs should be used. Technically, it takes fewer pounds of aluminum to do the bodywork of an automobile than it takes of steel. A technician may, for this reason, prefer aluminum to steel. The businessman would ask, "Which is the cheaper?" Suppose it takes two cubic feet of metal to make the body of the automobile. Suppose further that steel is three times as heavy per cubic foot as aluminum so that it takes 1,000 pounds of steel to cover the car but only 333 pounds of aluminum. Now, if aluminum cost $.25 a pound while steel costs only $.05 a pound, steel would be cheaper to use than aluminum. The steel cost is $50.00 (= 1000 × $.05), while the aluminum cost is $83.25 (= 333 × $.25). If the steel car sells for the same amount as the aluminum car, the businessman would minimize his costs and maximize his profits by using steel instead of aluminum.

Decisions which involve working an existing plant at different rates are called *short-run* decisions, and decisions which involve changing the number or size of plants are called *long-run* decisions. Short-run cost calculations are used to make short-run decisions. Short-run costs are calculated from the Law of Diminishing Returns because the Law of Diminishing Returns describes the behavior of output when an existing plant, which can be considered as the fixed factor, is worked at different rates. One input is fixed, while other inputs vary. Long-run costs, which are used to make long-run decisions, are calculated from returns to scale, because returns to scale describe the behavior of output when the size of plant is changed. All inputs vary.

The opportunity cost principle is used in making both short-run and long-run decisions. Short-run decisions set the rate of output for a plant. Should a factory produce 100 or 200 units a day? What is the cost at one rate of output and what is the cost at the other rate of output? Which rate of output gives the highest rate of profit? Long-run decisions determine whether a large or small plant should be built or whether any plant should be built at all. Should an entrepreneur build a factory which will produce 25,000 or 50,000 units a year? What are the alternative costs? What are the alternative profits? Should an entrepreneur go out of business and become a salaried employee? Which opportunity gives him the best return? In each case the businessman will choose the opportunity which gives him the greatest profit (or the least loss).

In the following discussion of cost, the entrepreneur is assumed to use the principle of opportunity cost to minimize his costs at each level of output, to determine the rate of output, to determine the scale of plant, and to determine whether he should be in business. This cost analysis is simplified in a number of ways. First, the enterprise is assumed to be a sole proprietorship which produces one output with two groups of inputs: a fixed group and a variable group. Second, the cost of production includes the opportunity cost of the proprietor because the services of the proprietor are necessary if production is to take place. The proprietor must be paid as much as he can get elsewhere and his pay is a cost of production. It is a fixed cost. The sense of this cost analysis is not changed when these assumptions are altered to fit more realistic cases.

Short-run costs

In the short run, the output of a firm is limited by the size of its existing plant. It can increase output by employing more men, but the period is too short to acquire or construct additional capacity. As output increases, costs per unit must eventually rise because of the law of diminishing returns. The law of diminishing returns states that equal increments of a variable input (labor), given at least one fixed input (land), will eventually cause output (corn) to increase at a diminishing rate. In other words, as expenditures on labor rise steadily, output rises, but eventually it does so at a falling rate. Thus, costs per unit output must eventually rise.

The cost of producing corn can be derived from Table 3-1. Suppose that laborers work in this field for one day a year at $5.00 a day and that an acre of land is rented for $1.50 a year. The cost of production can be calculated in three steps. Step 1: *total variable cost* equals the wage of labor multiplied by the quantity of labor used at each level of output. Step 2: *total fixed cost* equals the rent of an acre of land multiplied by the number of acres used. Step 3: the *total cost* of production at each level of output equals total variable cost plus total fixed cost. These calculations are made in Table 3-2, which repeats Table 3-1 in its first four columns.

The distinction between a fixed cost and a variable cost is not always clear. A variable cost (variable input) is one which varies because the level of output varies. A fixed cost (fixed input) is one which does *not* vary with the level of output. Whether a cost is fixed or variable depends upon its employment contract. In the current example it is assumed that the land is rented for at least a period of a year since that is the minimum time it can be used. It is assumed that labor is the variable cost since it can be used for shorter periods of time. However, in other cases, capital costs may vary and labor costs may be fixed. For example, computers can be rented by the second, but few statisticians or engineers would accept so short a contract.

In order to compare the cost of production to the price of the product, it is useful to calculate cost per unit or average cost. There are three categories of average cost which correspond to the three categories of total cost. *Average variable cost* (AVC) equals total

Table 3-2
The Calculation of Costs

I	II	III	IV	V	VI	VII	VIII	IX	X	XI
Variable Input	Fixed Input	Total Product	Marginal Product	Total Variable Cost	Total Fixed Cost	Total Cost	Average Variable Cost	Average Fixed Cost	Average Cost	Marginal Cost
Labor (days)	Land (acres)	Corn (bushels)	Corn (bushels)	($5.00 × I)	*($1.50 × II)	†(V + VI)	(V ÷ III)	(VI ÷ III)	(VIII + IX)	(Change in VII ÷ change in III)
0	5	0	2.0	$ 0	$7.50	$ 7.50	$0	$ –	$ –	$ 2.50
1	5	2.0	4.0	5.00	7.50	12.50	2.50	3.75	6.25	1.25
2	5	6.0	6.0	10.00	7.50	17.50	1.67	1.25	2.92	.83
3	5	12.0	7.0	15.00	7.50	22.50	1.25	.63	1.88	.71
4	5	19.0	6.0	20.00	7.50	27.50	1.05	.39	1.44	.83
5	5	25.0	5.0	25.00	7.50	32.50	1.00	.30	1.30	1.00
6	5	30.0	4.0	30.00	7.50	37.50	1.00	.25	1.25	1.25
7	5	34.0	3.0	35.00	7.50	42.50	1.03	.22	1.25	1.67
8	5	37.0	2.0	40.00	7.50	47.50	1.08	.20	1.28	2.50
9	5	39.0	1.0	45.00	7.50	52.50	1.15	.19	1.34	5.00
10	5	40.0	0.5	50.00	7.50	57.50	1.25	.19	1.44	10.00
11	5	40.5		55.00	7.50	62.50	1.36	.19	1.55	

* Price of labor = $5.00 a day.
† Price of land = $1.50 an acre.

variable cost divided by output. Average variable cost is U-shaped. At first it falls, but eventually it rises. *Average fixed cost* (AFC) equals total fixed cost divided by output. Since total fixed cost is constant, average fixed cost falls steadily as output increases, forming a rectangular hyperbola. Average total cost, or simply *average cost* (AC), equals average variable cost plus average fixed cost, or total cost divided by output. Its curve is shaped like an average variable cost curve. These calculations also appear in Table 3-2 and Figure 3-3.

The last cost category to be calculated is *marginal cost* (MC). *Marginal cost is the change in total cost associated with a change in output.* It is calculated by dividing the change in total cost by the change in output. Marginal cost is particularly useful in applying the principle of opportunity cost to output decisions. How much will an additional unit of business cost? Is it worth undertaking? How much will a cutback in production save?

Total Variable Cost = Quantity of Labor × Price of Labor.
Total Fixed Cost = Quantity of Land × Price of Land.
Total Cost = Total Variable Cost + Total Fixed Cost.
Average Variable Cost = Total Variable Cost ÷ Output
Average Fixed Cost = Total Fixed Cost ÷ Output
Average Cost = Average Variable Cost + Average Fixed Cost.
Marginal Cost = Change in Total Cost ÷ Change in Output

Average cost, average variable cost, and marginal cost are graphed in Figure 3-3. They have a definite relationship. Average fixed cost is the difference between average cost and average variable cost. AC = AVC + AFC. Notice that marginal cost falls over a considerable range of output before it turns up. It turns up because of the law of diminishing returns, that is, after 16 units of output, total output rises at a diminishing rate as the variable input rises by equal increments. Since less output is produced for each additional dollar spent on the variable input, the cost of additional output rises. As marginal cost rises, it eventually intersects average variable cost and then average cost at their minimum points. This is necessarily true, as can be seen from a moment's reflection on the more familiar problem of baseball batting averages. If a ballplayer is batting .300 at the start of a game, his average will fall if he bats below .300 and rise if he bats above .300. Similarly, where the addition to cost (marginal cost) is below the average, the average necessarily falls; and, where the addition to cost is above the average, the average rises. As marginal cost approaches average cost from below, average cost will fall by declining amounts. As soon as marginal cost exceeds average cost, average cost must rise. Therefore, marginal cost equals average cost, where average cost is at its minimum.

The minimum point on the average cost curve is the least-cost level of operation, though it may not be the most profitable level. The least-cost point is defined as *capacity* by economists. When output is below capacity, there is *excess capacity*.

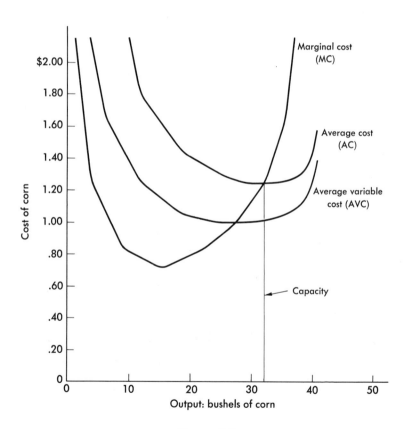

Figure 3-3.
Short-Run Cost Curves

The U-shaped cost curves in Figure 3-4 are not typical of all enterprises. Many businesses have cost curves shaped like those in Figure 3-4. At first, average cost falls rapidly as fixed costs are spread over a larger and larger volume of business. Then the average cost curve becomes nearly flat and remains flat until capacity is reached, after which it rises steeply.

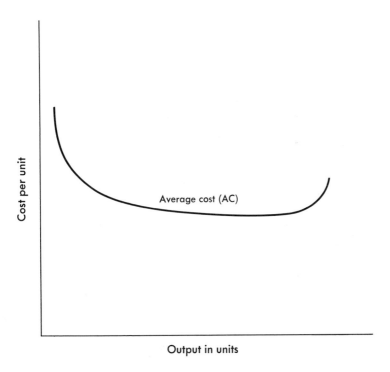

Figure 3-4.
Flat Short-Run Cost Curve

Long-run costs

Long-run decisions focus on the scale of operations. Long-run costs convert returns to scale into monetary terms. How efficient are different sized plants? Are large plants more, equally, or less costly to operate than small ones? That is, does an increase in all inputs yield increasing, constant, or decreasing returns to scale?

The long-run average cost (LRAC) curve traces the internal economies and diseconomies of scale.[5] These economies and diseconomies are called internal, because they take place within the firm as it changes size. In other words, long-run cost curves are derived from a series of alternative short-run cost curves. They fall with increasing returns, are horizontal with constant returns, and rise with decreasing returns to scale. The traditional U-shaped long-run average cost curve combines all three possibilities. At first, economies of scale reduce costs, at the very bottom of the curve, returns to scale are constant, and finally, diseconomies of scale cause costs to rise.

In Figure 3-5, Plant No. 1 (AC_1) has a higher minimum cost point than the larger plant No. 2 (AC_2). Plant No. 3 (AC_3), the largest plant, also has costs above those of Plant No. 2. Plant No. 2 is the least-cost plant. In addition to the plant AC curves drawn in Figure 3-5, there are plants smaller than AC_1, larger than AC_3, and all sizes in between. If the size of plants is increased little by little over the whole range of output, they trace out the long-run average cost curve in Figure 3-5. Since the long-run average cost curve shows the lowest possible cost of producing various levels of output, it is tangent to the lowest possible plant average cost curve at each level of output.

The least-cost point of a plant is not necessarily the least-cost at which that volume of output can be produced. To produce a given output, it may be cheaper to build a larger plant and operate it below capacity than it is to build a smaller plant and operate it at capacity. Thus, the minimum cost point of Plant No. 1 (AC_1) does not touch the long-run average cost curve. At the level of output

[5] External economies and diseconomies describe what happens to long-run costs of the firm when a whole industry expands or contracts. If there is a once-and-for-all outward shift in demand, an industry may experience constant costs, increasing costs, or decreasing costs as production increases. Two kinds of things might cause external costs to change. (1) Firms might bid up the price of a scarce input. For example: if farm land is scarce, the price of land may rise with an expansion in the demand for food, thus increasing costs. (2) The technical conditions of production might change. If an agricultural district were plagued by multiplying rabbits, one or a few farmers might not be able to combat them. The arrival of more farmers might make control possible, thus decreasing costs, even though each farmer looked after just his own interest.

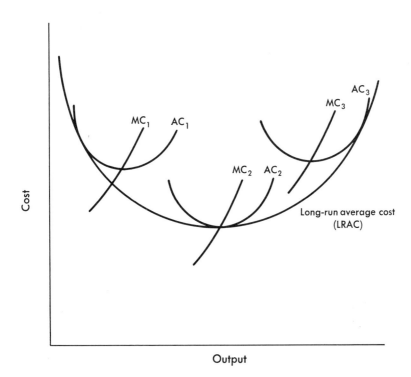

Figure 3-5.
Long-Run Average Cost Curve

where AC_1 is at its minimum, a somewhat larger plant can produce at a lower cost even though the larger plant does not operate at capacity.

The long-run curve is not necessarily U-shaped. The shape depends upon the facts of a particular situation. In some industries, firms become more and more efficient as they increase in size. If the giant firm is more efficient than the small one, the structure of the market may be affected. A competitive market—one where there are so many sellers that no one can influence the price—may become technically unfeasible. A *natural monopoly*—also called a technical monopoly—may arise where a single large firm can supply the whole market at lower costs than two or more smaller firms. This is often the case with local telephone, gas, water, and electric companies. If two companies were to string wires or lay pipes on every street in town, the cost would be exorbitant. One firm can supply the market at a lower price than two.

What the businessman or the accountant means by cost is not always what the economist means by cost. Economists distinguish between private costs and social costs. Private costs are costs to a private enterprise, whereas social costs include all costs. If a factory pollutes the air or a river in the process of making steel, the burden of the pollution is born by society, not by the steel company. The pollution is a real cost of the steel. It is a social cost paid by those individuals who breathe the foul air, who wash their clothes and paint their houses more frequently, and who travel farther to fish or swim or boat. Such a divergence between private and social cost is called a *neighborhood effect*. This term also applies to situations where private benefits and social benefits are unequal. The benefit to society from the work of an Einstein, a Hume, or a Keynes is far greater than the pecuniary reward received for such work.

4

Pure Competition

A purely competitive market is free of monopoly elements. It is free of those elements which restrict supply or distort demand. First, there are so many buyers and sellers that no one of them can significantly influence the equilibrium price. No single buyer is large enough to affect demand, and no individual seller is large enough to affect supply. Second, all buyers and sellers are transacting in identical or homogeneous products. No buyer has any reason to prefer the goods of one seller over those of another. If one seller were to raise his price above the market price, he would find no buyers. If one seller were to advertise in order to attract customers, he would be wasting his money. Buyers know that his product is identical to all the others. Third, anyone is free to enter the market either as a buyer or a seller.

Few markets are purely competitive. Agriculture was the best example of pure competition before the government intervened to bolster prices and incomes. In many agricultural markets, buyers and sellers number in the thousands or millions, and for all practical purposes the products are physically identical. Now, however, the government restricts entry into some markets, limits production or sales in others, and buys heavily in still others. The New York Stock

Exchange and the federal bond market are perhaps the most competitive markets in the United States today. Nevertheless, these markets are watched closely by the government to make sure they remain competitive. In the past, even the largest and most competitive markets were small enough for an occasional speculator to manipulate.

A distinction is often made between *pure* competition and *perfect* competition, though a market may be both purely and perfectly competitive. A perfectly competitive market possesses the abstract qualities of perfect mobility and perfect knowledge. In a perfect market, resources are so mobile that they can move freely from one place or from one industry to another, and buyers and sellers have such perfect knowledge that no transaction goes unnoticed. Even future transactions are assumed to be known.

The assumption of perfect competition simplifies the analysis of markets. It permits economists to carry the analysis of market forces to an equilibrium point, though in fact imperfections retard the movement toward equilibrium. In reality, the North Dakota wheat farmer cannot easily switch to other crops when wheat becomes unprofitable. Similarly, the Pennsylvania coal miner cannot easily find work as a machinist or carpenter when the coal mines close. However, if the profits or wages which can be earned in one market are sufficiently greater than what can be earned in another, resources will tend to move toward the higher income market. Also, few buyers and sellers actually keep track of the hourly variations in prices, and few can predict the future course of prices, but there are frequently enough well-informed traders to assure the orderly operation of the market. In the following discussion it is assumed that markets are purely and perfectly competitive.

The *equilibrium* level of prices, the level towards which prices tend, depends upon the period of time during which a given set of forces have to work themselves out. If there is an unexpected shift in demand, the immediate impact on prices may be quite different from the final result. For this reason economists have divided the analysis of time into three periods: the market period, the short run, and the long run. This tripartite analysis of time, like many other useful tools in price theory, was developed by Alfred Marshall.[1]

[1] Alfred Marshall, *Principles of Economics* (London: Macmillan, 1959), pp. 269–291; originally published in 1890.

The Market Period

In the market period, supply is limited to the stock of goods on hand. Current production cannot alter supply. Chapter 1—Elementary Supply and Demand—dealt with market period problems. The market period is used to analyze the behavior of prices in markets (1) where production is periodic (such as agriculture), (2) where current production is small relative to the accumulated stock on hand (such as gold mining or residential construction), or (3) where further production is not possible (such as rare coins, art masterpieces, or land).

The supply of agricultural goods, for example, can only be changed once a year. After farmers have planted their seed, relatively little can be done to change the volume or composition of farm output. People must simply wait for the next year's planting and harvest. The market period for agriculture lasts many months. This is not true of manufacturing because manufacturing is virtually a continuous process. It is possible to increase or decrease the output of steel, automobiles, or cement on relatively short notice.

Agricultural prices are notoriously less stable than other prices, partly because supply can only be changed once a year. This is illustrated by the behavior of prices at the beginning of the Korean War. The start of the war in June 1950 caused a sudden increase in demand. This was due partly to speculative and panic buying and partly to the needs of the war. Agricultural prices responded by rising 22.8% between June 1950 and March 1951, while other prices rose only 15.9% during the same period, according to the Wholesale Price Index (WPI) of the Bureau of Labor Statistics (BLS). After March 1951, farm prices started to fall, and they continued to fall thereafter. Both the rise and fall in agricultural prices must have corresponded primarily to a rise and fall in demand since there had not been time to change output. The movement of agricultural prices took place within the market period.

Supply is not the same in the market period as it is in the short run and the long run, because in the short run and the long run, the quantity supplied is directly related to the cost of production. In the market period price may be far above or far below the cost of production. Demand may shift from peacetime to wartime levels, but the quantity supplied cannot exceed the stock of goods on hand.

The Short Run

In the short run, output can range from zero to the physical limits set by the existing plant and equipment. The actual rate of output is determined by the sum of all the individual firms in the market acting separately. Each firm decides how much it will produce by comparing its costs with the market price.

Competitive markets are impersonal—no individual person can influence them. There are so many buyers and sellers that no one of them can significantly affect the market price. The individual firm can sell all it wants at the going price, because it is so small it cannot influence the price. For example, the Kansas wheat farmer takes the price as set in the market, and he cannot change it. The market price is, then, the demand curve facing the individual firm.

In Figure 4-1, the demand curve for the individual firm is drawn as a horizontal line, indicating that the price does not change no matter how much the individual firm sells. The market price changes when the market supply curve or the market demand curve shifts, but it takes many individuals acting in concert to shift the market schedule. If consumers in general lose their taste for bread, the price of wheat will fall. If the market price changes, the demand curve facing the firm also changes. A fall in price shifts the firm's demand curve down. A rise in price shifts the firm's demand curve up.

The demand curve of the firm is also its marginal revenue curve. The marginal revenue curve measures the change in total revenue associated with a change in the quantity sold. When the demand curve is horizontal, every unit is sold at the same price. Additional sales are made at the same price. Therefore, the additional revenue derived from selling one more unit is simply the price of that unit.

Supply in the short run is determined by the short-run cost curves. If the individual firm wants to maximize its profits, it will adjust its output to that level where total revenue exceeds total cost by the largest possible amount. How does the firm know when its profits are at a maximum? It looks at its marginal revenue and marginal cost curves. If marginal revenue is greater than marginal cost, profits can be increased by increasing output, because the addition to revenue will exceed the addition to cost. Profits must rise if revenue rises more than costs. If marginal cost exceeds marginal revenue, profits are increased by decreasing output. Costs fall more than revenue, therefore profits rise. Where marginal revenue equals marginal cost, profits are at a maximum. If output is at any other point, profits can be increased by changing output.

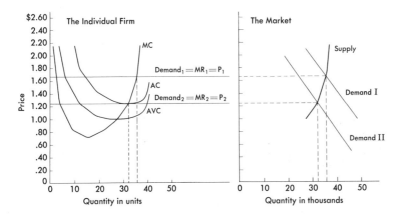

Figure 4-1.
Short-Run Equilibrium for the Firm and in the Market

Remember the rule for *profit maximization:* MC = MR.

The principle that profits are maximized where MC = MR can be demonstrated by referring back to Table 3-2. If price (and therefore individual demand and marginal revenue) equals $2.50, production would be carried to the interval between 37 and 39 units, the interval to which the marginal cost of $2.50 applies. Actually, the profit is the same for both 37 and 39 bushels of output. Where costs are continuous functions, this ambiguity does not exist. At 39 bushels, total revenue = $97.50 ($2.50 × 39), total cost = $52.50, and net profit = $45.00. If production is carried beyond this point, profits fall. When 40 bushels are produced, total revenue = $100.00, total cost = $57.50, and net profit = $42.50. If production is reduced to 34 bushels, profits also fall. Total revenue = $85.00, total cost = $42.50, net profit = $42.50. Profits are maximized where MC = MR.

The marginal cost curve is the supply curve for the firm. As price moves up and down, the firm maximizes its profits by adjusting its output along the marginal cost schedule. In Figure 4-1, which graphs the data in Table 3-2 as continuous curves, the individual firm supplies 38 (between 37 and 39) bushels when the price is $2.50, 32 bushels when the price is $1.25, and 27½ bushels when the price is $1.00.

When price falls below $1.00, the firm will stop producing. It will not be covering costs it could avoid by shutting down its plant. Below $1.00 a unit, the variable input is costing more than the revenue it produces. The firm can reduce its losses by dismissing workers, stopping purchases, and leaving its plant idle. When it is not producing, its only cost is its fixed cost. Why buy something for more than you can sell it? The point where price equals average variable cost is the *shut-down point*. Since the profit maximizing firm will stop supplying at prices below its average variable cost, the supply curve for the firm is just that portion of the marginal cost curve which is above the shut-down point.

Why doesn't the firm shut down its plant when price falls below average cost (AC)? If it shuts down, it still has its fixed costs, but it has no revenue at all. Any revenue which the firm can earn in excess of its variable costs will cover part of its fixed costs. Instead of running at a loss equal to its total fixed cost, it will run at a smaller loss. Thus, when price per unit is above variable cost per unit (AVC), it pays to keep producing.

The sum of all individual supply curves is the market supply curve. The market supply curve in Figure 4-1 equals the sum of 1,000 identical individual supply curves. As the market demand curve shifts up and down, marginal production becomes more or less profitable; and all firms increase or decrease output. At $2.50, it is most profitable for each firm, acting independently, to supply 38 bushels. Together the firms supply the market with 38,000 bushels. When the price falls to $1.67, each firm produces 35.5 bushels; and the market is supplied with 35,500 units. Thus, in the short run, output adjusts to shifts in demand.

In the short run, price may be greater than, equal to, or less than the average cost of production (AC). When price equals average cost, the firm is at its *break-even point*. At this point all the costs of production are covered, including the opportunity cost of the businessman's services, that is, including as much income as the businessman could earn in his next best alternative opportunity. This is sometimes called a "normal" profit. In Figure 4-2 when price is above $1.25, the firm is earning an *excess profit*. When price is below $1.25, the firm is operating at a *loss*.

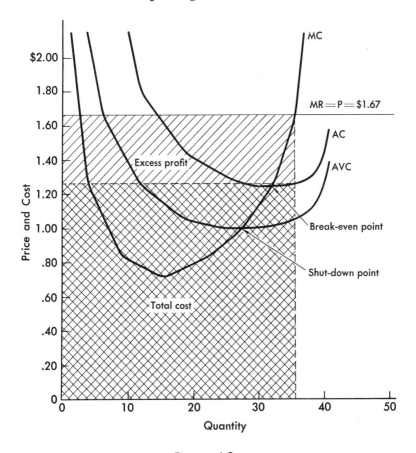

Figure 4-2.
Short-Run Cost and Profit

In the short run, there is no tendency for excess profits or losses to be eliminated. The limit to supply is set by the productive capacity of the industry. In the short run, both the size and number of firms is fixed. On the one hand, whenever productive capacity is insufficient, excess profits are earned. On the other hand, whenever productive capacity is excessive, losses are incurred.

The Long Run

In the long run, firms can enter or leave the industry, plant and equipment can be constructed or depreciated. If excess profits exist in an industry, new firms will be attracted to it. Productive capacity will be increased, the market supply schedule will shift out, and price will be forced down. If losses exist in an industry, firms will be forced out of business, the market supply will shift in, and the price will rise. Both the excess profits that attract new business and the losses that bankrupt old business regulate production. The entry and exit of firms eliminates excess profits and losses.

The long-run price tends to equal the *least-cost point* on the long-run average cost curve, provided all firms have the same costs. When the price is above this point, any firm can temporarily make excess profits by building a plant whose average cost curve dips below the prevailing price. Any businessman who does not adopt the most efficient scale plant will eventually be forced out of business or be forced to accept a lower income than he could get elsewhere.

Figure 4-3 illustrates the tendency of price to fall to the least-cost point of the most efficient scale plant. If for any reason each firm in an industry found that its plant (AC_1) was smaller than the most efficient scale plant (AC_2), and if the market price (P_1) were above the equilibrium level, any firm could temporarily earn excess profits by building a larger plant (say, AC_2). However, as excess profits stimulate more and more firms to build larger plants, the market supply curve shifts out, price falls, and excess profits disappear. With perfect foresight only the least-cost plant would be built.

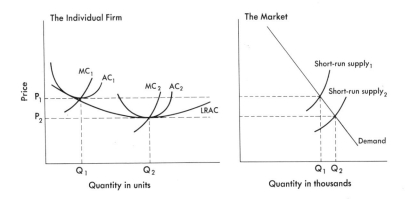

Figure 4-3.
Long-Run Equilibrium for the Firm and in the Market

If the somewhat unrealistic proviso that all firms have the same costs is removed, the long-run analysis is less precise but the gist of the argument is the same. If some businessmen have superior entrepreneurial talents, they will tend to earn profits in excess of the industry average year after year. Inferior entrepreneurs will earn less than the average. However, the average businessman who enters the industry can only expect to earn "normal" profits.

Two Applications

Price theory is a *static theory* which explains the tendency toward one equilibruim point at a time. It does not explain why consumers change their minds and shift their demands from one product to another. It does not explain why technology changes. However, once a change is known to have taken place, once the new equilibrium point is known, price theory can be used to analyze the new equilibrium adjustment. An analysis which compares one static equilibrium with another is called *comparative statics*.

A shift in demand

Let us assume that there is a once-and-for-all shift in demand from meat to fish. Let us further assume that all the relevant markets are purely competitive and that they all had previously been operating at their long-run equilibrium level—at their least-cost volume. Finally, assume all firms have identical U-shaped cost curves.

The fall in the demand for meat is noticed first by retailers who cut back their purchases from meat packers. Meat packers, in turn, reduce their demand for cattle and hogs. The fall in the demand for livestock forces their prices down sharply. Farmers and ranchers who have spent years building up their herds now find that their herds are excessive. Because of the fall in demand, they can only sell their stock well below the cost of production. They can hold their cattle off the market, but they cannot sell them for a profit. In the market period they cannot adjust their current production to demand.

Neither retailers nor meat packers are likely to be caught with excessive stocks in the market period, because their inventories typically equal only a few days' sales. They are left with excess capacity at the new level of demand. Since they were previously assumed to be operating at their most efficient volume and just breaking even, they are now operating below capacity and not covering all their costs. At the new short-run equilibrium, average cost exceeds marginal cost; and competition drives the price down to marginal cost. Thus, average cost exceeds the price, and the retailers and packers operate at a loss.

In the short run, breeders and feeders can work off their excessive stocks and reduce their rate of production to a more profitable level. The prices of cattle and hogs will tend to rise from their initial low point, but they will not rise enough to cover average cost. At the new level of demand, there are simply too many producers. Supply is so large that price is depressed below the break-even point.

In the long run, excess capacity is eliminated. Enough meat markets, packers, farmers, and ranchers go out of business or transfer to another business to reduce supply and raise the price. The new long-run equilibrium price, like the old, will be at the minimum point on the long-run average cost curve. It will be just high enough to compensate businessmen for their services.

In the fish industry the opposite forces are at work. Demand shifts outward, so that prices tend to rise. Fish markets, fish canners, and fishermen all make excess profits. These excess profits draw resources into the fish industry. In the long run, enough new companies, workers, equipment, and supplies enter the industry to increase supply, depress price, and reduce profits to the equilibrium level. Since it is ultimately the profits that allocate resources in a free enterprise economy, the reduction of profits to the equilibrium level stops the flow of additional resources into the fish industry.

Technological change

Let us assume that an inventor develops a new harvesting machine, one that is far more efficient than any of its predecessors and allows one farmer to do the work of three at half his previous cost. Let us also assume that all relevant markets are purely competitive, that they were at their long-run equilibrium before the invention was made, and that all firms have U-shaped cost curves.

This new harvester lowers the cost and increases the scale of the most efficient farm. The first farmers who buy and use this machine earn excess profits on their old acreage, and they are encouraged to increase it. When other farmers see the large profits that their neighbors are earning, they, too, adopt the new way. As more farmers cultivate additional land and as new farmers enter farming, the supply shifts out and price falls. In this way the benefits of the invention are passed on to the public.

But everything is not so rosy. Fewer farmers are required to grow the same quantities of goods. If land is limited or if demand is inelastic, some farmers will be forced out of business. It will not be possible for every farmer to expand to the most efficient scale. Those who act quickly, adopt the new technology, and add acreage to their farms will drive price below the costs of those who move more slowly. Those who enter last must either find other work or accept lower incomes.

Technological change has often caused fundamental changes in the structure of society. The development of the automobile, for example, radically changed the nature of American society. The suburb, the shopping plaza, and the superhighway are all by-products of the automobile industry. These things, however, take us well beyond static price theory.

The Political Economy of Pure Competition

In his *Wealth of Nations* (1776), Adam Smith pleaded persuasively that private competition directed economic activity more effectively than public regulation, that the private vice of profit-seeking guided by the "invisible hand" of competition led to the public virtue of maximum material welfare.[2] Many economists, social philosophers, and politicians have advocated since that the government should take every step possible to establish and maintain a highly competitive system. According to this point of view, pure competition is ideal. It is the standard by which other systems should be measured since under pure competition, (1) resources are properly allocated, (2) income is distributed according to productiveness, and (3) invention is encouraged and its fruits are passed on to the public.

Proper resource allocation is separate from the question of optimal income distribution. Income distribution is discussed at greater length in Chapter 9. Proper resource allocation means (1) that total output is the maximum which is technically possible with given resources, and (2) that the composition of output gives consumers a maximum satisfaction from their incomes.

Within the individual firm, output is the greatest which is technically possible with given resources. To maximize its profits, the individual firm must minimize its costs. To minimize its costs, it must combine its resources in the most efficient manner possible. In the absence of competition, however, the individual firm may use too few or too many resources.

Within a purely competitive industry, a given set of resources is allocated among the firms so that total output for the industry is

[2] Adam Smith, *The Wealth of Nations* (New York: Random House, 1937).

maximized. In a purely competitive industry, each firm maximizes its profits by setting output where MC = P. Since only a single price can prevail in a competitive industry, the MC of every firm equals the MC of every other firm. This equality of MC's implies that total output is at its maximum and that the transfer of resources to one firm from another will decrease total output. The proof of this proposition is the following. The MC of each firm rises as output increases because of the law of diminishing returns. Each additional unit of input yields a smaller addition to output. If a given quantity of resources is transferred to a first firm from a second firm, the MC of the first firm rises because its last dose of resources produces a smaller increase in total output than did its previous dose. The MC of the second firm falls for a similar reason. Its last dose of resources now produces more than before. Before the transfer, both firms produced the same additional output from their last dose of resources. As a result of the transfer, the output of the first firm rises less than the output of the second firm falls. Therefore, total output within the industry is at the maximum possible from its given set of resources when the MC of each firm equals the market price. If the economy is not competitive, however, a competitive industry may use too few or too many resources.

Within an economy of purely competitive industries, each enterprise maximizes its profits where MC = P, but different prices exist in different industries. This equality of MC and P in every industry implies that the value of total output for the economy is maximized. If resources are transferred to a first industry from a second industry, the value of total output will fall without changing total cost. The addition to total output in the first industry valued at its price will be smaller than the subtraction from total output in the second industry valued at its price. This is because the marginal product in the first industry will fall while the marginal product in the second industry will rise. In other words, pure competition puts the economy on its production possibilities frontier.

Proper resource allocation is not just a matter of maximizing the output from scarce resources. It is also a matter of consumer preferences. A purely competitive economy can produce any combination of outputs efficiently. To maximize social welfare, it must produce what consumers demand.

Individual consumers will, in their own self-interest, demand that combination of outputs that maximizes their satisfaction. When the individual consumer is free to choose those products which he prefers, he will maximize his well-being by applying the equal marginal principle. He will be certain that the last dollar he spends on every product gives him an equal amount of additional utility. If he receives a greater utility from the last dollar of hamburgers than from the last dollar of hot dogs, he will be better off if he buys more hamburgers and fewer hot dogs. When he can no longer increase his material welfare by purchasing more of one thing or less of another, his material welfare will be at its maximum. It is at its maximum when the marginal utility relative to the price of each good is the same.

The individual consumer demands those products that maximize his satisfaction, given his preferences, his income, and prices. The sum of individual demand curves is the market demand curve. The individual entrepreneur supplies that quantity of output which maximizes his profit, given technology and prices. The sum of individual supply curves is the market supply curve. Prices are determined simultaneously when supply and demand meet in the market. Under pure competition, those prices bring forth the maximum possible output and give consumers the maximum possible satisfaction. In other words, consumers are on the highest possible indifference curve that society's production possibilities curve will permit.[3]

It has already been shown in the case of profits that, under pure competition, businessmen earn no monopoly or excess income. In the long run they receive just as much profit as is necessary to induce them to carry out production, no more, no less. Chapter 9 will develop the proposition that income is distributed to the factors of production in proportion to the market value of the goods they produce.

[3] Some hidden assumptions are in this analysis that could seriously alter the conclusion. Most important, when all consumers are considered at the same time, it is necessary to assume that they have similar preferences. If their preferences differ, some consumers could be made better off and others worse off by changing the composition of output. If one person is made better off at the expense of another, who can say whether society is better off? For this reason, welfare economists have a special and limited meaning of maximum material welfare, called the *Pareto optimum* (named after the economist Vilfredo Pareto). The Pareto optimum exists when *no one can be made better off without making someone else worse off.*

Innovation is stimulated by the prospect of making temporary excess profits. Any businessman who introduces a cost-saving invention earns excess profits, until enough competitors have copied him to increase supply and depress prices. The fall in prices gives consumers the permanent benefit of the invention. Patents are incompatible with a purely competitive system. They are monopoly grants, preventing competitors from copying an invention.

No private enterprise economy is purely competitive. Indeed, many people, who have nothing but the good of society in mind, do not think any economy ever could or should be purely competitive. They support their position with a variety of reasons.

First, economies of large scale production may create natural monopolies. In many industries the most efficient scale of plant is so large relative to the size of the market that only one or two firms are needed to produce the quantity demanded at the minimum cost of production. Smaller firms would simply be driven out of business because of their higher costs. Where important economies of large scale production exist, pure competition can only exist if plants are smaller than the most efficient scale. Under pure competition, there must be so many sellers that no one of them can influence the price. In the American steel, aluminum, and cement industries, to name only a few, it is possible for one large firm to break the market price at will. These industries are oligopolies and are discussed in Chapter 7.

Second, most manufacturing and retailing companies sell differentiated products, such as automobiles, clothing, and whiskey. Where products are differentiated, pure competition can not exist. Pure competition assumes that products are homogeneous. Differentiated products attract loyal customers who are willing to pay more for their favorite brand than for close substitutes. This is one of the chief characteristics of a monopolistically competitive market. As will be seen in Chapter 6, monopolistic competition differs from pure competition.

Third, the long run may be too long. It may take too long or involve too great a sacrifice for unemployed coal miners or small scale farmers to find new occupations.

Some industries may never approach the long run. This is especially true in an economy that suffers from cyclical fluctuations in demand and that operates at or near capacity only when it is at the peak of the business cycle or at war. Under these conditions, competitive industries are stimulated to expand when demand is strong; but they must endure excess capacity, low prices, and low incomes the rest of the time. It may take only a few years to build up plant and equipment in an industry. It may take even less time to induce young workers to commit their lives to a particular trade or profession. Once these decisions have been made, they are not easily reversed. Businessmen and workers may be forced to accept low incomes for a great many years before excess capacity in the industry is eliminated. Yet, before prices approach the long-run equilibrium level, another short-lived spurt in demand starts the whole process over again. This is a classic example of *destructive competition,* competition which produces chronically low incomes. World War I and World War II inflicted this kind of competition on agriculture, bituminous coal mining, and other industries.

In a similar way, industries that go through extended periods of technological change may suffer from destructive competition. Most of the time most of the firms may be too small to make "normal profits," while relatively few firms steadily adopt more and more efficient methods of production, increase supply, and push price down further and further. This has also been happening in agriculture and bituminous coal mining.

J. M. Clark has pointed out in his *Economics of Overhead Costs* (1923) that destructive competition is particularly severe in industries where fixed costs are a large part of total costs.[4] In such industries the gap between the shut-down point and the break-even point is large. A large gap means that high fixed cost industries will accept large losses before they shut down.

Fourth, critics of the private market system have often stated that market demand does not accurately reflect social benefit and that private costs do not represent social sacrifices. There are several reasons why social and market value might diverge.

In some cases, consumers do not act in their own self-interest, as viewed by society. Some consumers do not have the mental capacity to recognize their self-interest. For this reason the law has long limited the right of children, morons, and drunks to contract freely. A small child who inherits a fortune might want a swimming

---

[4] J. M. Clark, *Studies in the Economic of Overhead Costs* (Chicago: University of Chicago Press, 1923), pp. 7–11.

pool of soda pop, a sandbox of sugar, and a bed of cotton candy. When the child grows up, he would probably regret having made these expenditures.

In some cases consumers do not have enough information to act in their own self-interest. Their knowledge is imperfect. Certainly few consumers can prescribe medicine for themselves when they are sick. Similarly, before the Food and Drug Act was passed, cosmetics and prepared foods often turned out to be highly poisonous. The individual consumer could not find out which products were poisonous and which were not. Even if he were a chemist and knew how to test for poisons, he probably would not have time to do so. Today, many consumers unknowingly pay exorbitant interest charges because they do not know how to calculate interest, do not have the time, or do not know where they can borrow for less.

In other cases private markets conceal substantial *neighborhood effects*. Water and air pollution are social costs that are rarely paid for by the enterprise which causes the pollution. If a city upstream dumps sewage and industrial wastes into a river, some city downstream may be forced to pay extraordinary costs to purify the water. The city upstream makes the city downstream pay for its sewage treatment. In such cases private costs are unrelated to social costs.

J. K. Galbraith [5] and many before him have argued that private individuals do not spend enough money on *public goods*. Free markets certainly can not be expected to look after public health and sanitation or to develop systems of streets and highways. In modern times, private markets do not and probably can not devote sufficient resources to education, scientific research, urban redevelopment, or mass transportation. Galbraith recommends that the government should expand the scope and magnitude of its economic activity in all these areas.

Fifth, J. A. Schumpeter [6] spent much of his life developing the hypothesis that monopolistic markets promote technical progress and economic growth more effectively than purely competitive markets. Agriculture and coal mining do not set the pace in today's economy. Chemicals, electronics, and aerospace are the dynamic

[5] J. K. Galbraith, *The Affluent Society* (Boston: Houghton Mifflin, 1958).
[6] J. A. Schumpeter, *Capitalism, Socialism and Democracy* (New York: Harper & Row, 1950), pp. 87–106; originally published in 1942.

industries in the American economy and all of these industries contain significant monopolistic elements. Schumpeter believed that the prospect of large monopoly profits stimulated innovation more effectively than the threat of minimal competitive profits. Monopoly, he argued, promotes the wealth of nations more surely than does pure competition.

5

Monopoly

A *monopoly* is a market in which there is only one seller. In the purest sense, a monopolist has no competitors at all. He is isolated from other markets. No one can deprive him of his customers by offering them lower prices. In reality, such a pure monopoly does not exist, but there are some markets that approach it.

For practical purposes, a monopoly is said to exist whenever the product of one firm has no close substitutes, whenever cross elasticity is close to zero. For example, local electric power companies have a virtual monopoly of home lighting. They do face potential competition from home generators, kerosene lamps, candles, and so on, but they could raise their prices very high before many customers would adopt such substitutes. Not all the electricity that power companies produce is sold under conditions of monopoly. While there are no close substitutes for electric lighting, there are close substitutes for electric heating (oil, gas, coal), cooking (gas), and hot water (gas). If the price of electricity rises relative to the price of gas, customers will tend to use more gas and less electricity for heating, cooking, and hot water.

Monopoly Equilibrium

A monopoly is in equilibrium when it maximizes its profits. To maximize profits, it fixes its output and sets its price where $MR = MC$, just as other firms do. If it stopped short of the point where $MR = MC$, marginal revenue would exceed marginal cost. By producing one more unit, it would add more to revenue than to cost. Thus, profits would rise (or losses would fall). As long as marginal revenue exceeds marginal cost, more is added to revenue than to cost as output expands. If it goes beyond the point $MR = MC$, it adds more to cost than to revenue and reduces its profit. Where $MR = MC$, profits are maximized.

In Figure 5-1, the demand curve for the monopolist is the demand curve for the whole market, since the monopolist is the only seller. The demand curve obeys the law of demand and slopes downward to the right. Consumers buy more as the price is lowered. The marginal revenue curve is related to the market demand curve. Marginal revenue falls more rapidly than demand because the monopolist reduces the price it gets on every unit it sells when it lowers its price enough to sell one more unit. It gains revenue because it sells one more unit, but it loses revenue because it sells its previous output at a lower price. Thus, the addition to revenue (MR) it receives is less than the price it gets for the extra unit of sales.

The graphic presentation of costs curves under monopoly is not exactly the same as it is under pure competition. A single graph is conventionally used to represent either the short-run or long-run situation. Since both the short-run and long-run curves are U-shaped, two separate graphs are not needed. It should be remembered, however, that the long-run average cost curve is made up of a series of short-run curves, which can be superimposed on it.

In Figure 5-1 the equilibrium price (P_1) is above the average cost of production (AC_1), so that the firm makes an excess profit on every unit it sells. The equilibrium rate of output (Q_1) is below the capacity rate of output in the short run and the size of the plant is below the most efficient scale in the long run. Neither price nor production are at the least-cost point.

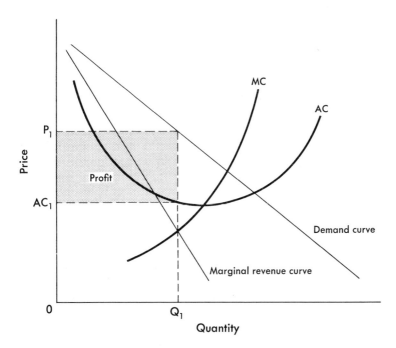

Figure 5-1.
Monopoly Equilibrium

Not all monopolists make excess profits. Some may just break even. In the short run, others may operate at a loss. In a depression, the demand curve facing a monopolist could temporarily fall below the average cost curve. See Figure 5-2. In such a depressed situation, the monopolist would produce at the point (Q_1) where MC = MR and set a price (P_1) to minimize its losses. If demand fell below average variable cost, the firm would shut down because variable inputs would not pay for themselves. In the long run, however, monopolists, like pure competitors, will go out of business if they do not at least break even, although they may earn excess profits. There will be no tendency for excess profits to be eliminated by competition, because there is no competition.

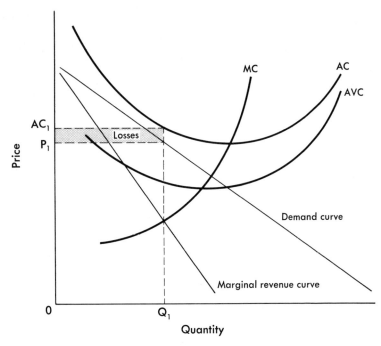

Figure 5-2.
Short-Run Losses under Monopoly

Monopoly and Public Policy

The private interest of a monopolist and the public interest of society do not always coincide. In contrast to purely competitive markets, there is no tendency for price to equal the cost of production or for output to be at the most efficient rate. Public policy, therefore, generally attempts to limit excessive monopoly power which restricts production.

It is frequently asserted that the monopoly price is higher than the competitive price and that the monopoly output is smaller than the competitive output, though this assertion is not easily proven. Monopoly markets must be comparable to purely competitive markets in order to make this proof. Clearly, a local telephone company which enjoys a "natural" monopoly can provide telephone service at a lower price than can a large number of competing telephone companies with wastefully duplicated equipment. The *economies of scale* enjoyed by a *natural monopoly* may more than offset the effect which the monopoly has when it restricts output and raises price.

If an industry is competitive to start with and if it is then organized into a monopoly, the monopoly of many small plants will tend to charge a higher price than the competitive market of many independent firms. Similarly, if a market is not purely competitive, but is an oligopoly, and if it is organized into a monopoly, the monopolist would probably raise the price. However, if the monopolist can lower cost by eliminating duplicative operations, the monopolist could conceivably lower prices.

Tradition divides monopolies into two groups: (1) "natural" monopolies, those which exist because one firm can supply the market at a lower price than two or more firms; and (2) "artificial" monopolies, those which exist because one firm controls a strategic resource, uses predatory tactics, colludes with all its competitors, or for some other reason. In the United States, the market power of "natural" monopolies is usually limited by regulation (private power companies and gas transmission pipelines) or by state ownership (the U.S. Post Office and TVA); while the market power of "artificial" monopolies is limited by the antitrust laws which promote competition.

Public control of natural monopolies

When the state regulates or owns a monopoly, it must decide what price to set. Price theory can aid in determining what price to set. It can trace out the implications of a pricing policy, but it can not say which policy best suits the public. As in other matters of public policy, there is more than one view of what suits the public. The monopolist has one view, his customers have another. In the following sections, three different pricing policies will be considered: marginal cost pricing, average cost pricing, and discriminatory pricing.

Marginal cost pricing is recommended by A. C. Pigou, *The*

Economics of Welfare (1920),[1] and by other economists. They recommend that price be set where the marginal cost curve intersects the demand curve. In other words, the monopoly price should do what the market price does in pure competition. Price should maximize social welfare, as valued by the market. Where price equals marginal cost, the amount that people are willing to pay for the last unit of output just equals the cost of producing the last unit of output. If output were increased, marginal cost would rise above price. The additional sacrifice (cost) would exceed the additional benefit (demand), as valued by the market. Society would gain, if output were cut back to the point where $MC = P$. Similarly, if output were restricted below the point where $MC = P$, the additional cost from increasing output would be below the additional benefit, as valued by the market. Social welfare would be increased by increasing output. The phrase "as valued by the market" must be emphasized, because the market value may not accurately reflect the social value, as Einstein's salary did not accurately reflect his contribution to society or as the private cost of making steel does not cover the social cost of air and water pollution.

Marginal cost pricing faces one theoretical problem that is also a political problem. The point at which the marginal cost curve intersects the demand curve may be above or below the average cost curve. In the first case, when the demand curve cuts the marginal cost curve above the average cost curve, price is above the average cost of doing business, so that the monopolist would earn excess profits. If a regulatory commission allowed a monopoly to earn excess profits, it would be called a double-dealer and a pawn in the hands of monopoly.

In the second case, when the demand curve cuts the marginal cost curve below the average cost curve, price is below average cost. The monopolist would not cover all its costs. It would not cover its *residual cost*, defined as the amount by which average cost exceeds marginal cost. In Figure 5-3, for example, the demand curve cuts the marginal cost curve below the average cost curve. Price (P_1) is below average cost (AC_1) so that the enterprise does not cover its residual costs $(AC_1 - P_1)$ and hence operates at a loss. Monopolists are not in business for losses, and they will not operate unless profits are in sight.

[1] A. C. Pigou, *The Economics of Welfare* (London: Macmillan, 1960), originally published in 1920.

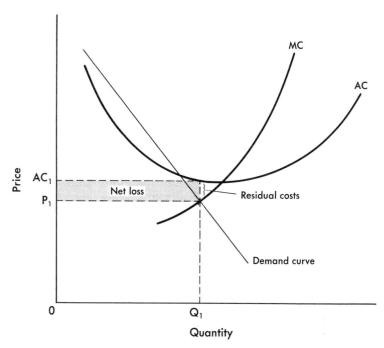

Figure 5-3.
Marginal Cost Pricing for a Monopoly

To solve this problem, A. C. Pigou recommended that the enterprise be paid a bounty (subsidized) in case price is below average cost, and that it be taxed in case price is above average cost. In Figure 5-3 the bounty would equal the net loss. In this way, the state would make sure that the enterprise continues in operation without earning excess profits. This plan has not been accepted by legislators, because the public believes in the principle that all enterprises, public and private, should cover their operating costs with their operating revenues, and if possible, enterprises should operate at a profit.

Even if the public supported the idea of marginal cost pricing in principle, it would oppose the payment of more taxes in practice. In many cases, the amount of money involved would be quite large. Consider what it costs to make one more telephone call, once the equipment is installed. Consider what it costs to haul one more

passenger from New York to Chicago, once the track is laid and the
train is ready. What does it cost the post office to deliver one more
letter? In all these cases marginal cost pricing would yield little
revenue most of the time. Perhaps most of the revenue of the telephone, railroad, and electric power companies would have to be
subsidy.

Average cost pricing is followed by many government enterprises and regulatory commissions. When price is set where the
average cost curve cuts the demand curve, the enterprise breaks
even and earns a normal profit, but social welfare may not be maximized. In Figure 5-4, price (P_1) is set equal to average cost, but
it exceeds marginal cost. The break-even point, where $P = AC$,
includes a "normal" profit.

In the United States, the law requires regulatory agencies to

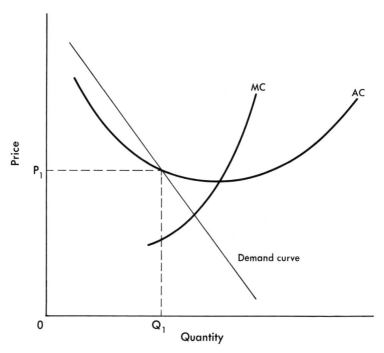

Figure 5-4.
Average Cost Pricing for a Monopoly

set prices high enough to assure businesses a "fair return" on their investment. This is a form of average cost pricing, but it leaves some unanswered questions. What rate of return is a "fair" rate? And how should invested capital be valued in order to calculate a "fair return"?

The rate of return must be sufficient to attract new capital into the industry. If it is below this rate, the industry will wither and the public will not be served. If the rate is much above this, the resources in the industry will earn more than they can earn elsewhere. They will earn a monopoly income.

Investment in productive facilities can be valued in at least three ways: (1) by capitalized earning value, (2) by replacement or reproduction cost, (3) by original or historical cost. First, valuing at capitalized earning power means valuing plant and equipment according to the profits they earn. If a 100,000 kilowatt generator earns more in Brooklyn, New York, than it does in Brooklyn, Iowa, the New York generator would be valued at a higher dollar amount than the Iowa generator. When the capital is valued according to profitability, the "fair return" differs little from what the unregulated monopolist earns. Yet, this sort of "regulation" exists in some areas.

Secondly, valuation by current cost of replacement or reproduction means valuation of both old and new plant and equipment according to new prices. This permits companies to earn windfall profits when the price of new equipment rises. For example, suppose a generating plant was built in 1932 at a cost of $1,000,000. Today it might cost as much as $4,000,000 to replace. If the capital is valued at replacement cost, the company would earn, say 6%, on $4,000,000 or $240,000 a year. This is a 24% return on their original cost. Such profits are unrelated to the cost of the service performed and, therefore, is probably not in the public interest. In addition, it would be nearly impossible to value old equipment which is no longer manufactured in current prices, for no prices exist for such equipment.

Finally, valuation at original or historical cost means valuation at the prices actually paid. It has two advantages: it does not permit windfall profits or losses and it is an existing market and accounting figure. Today, original cost is the most widely used method of capital valuation.

Discriminatory pricing means charging different rates to different customers for the same good or service. This is complicated by the fact that the cost of service to one group of customers may differ from the cost of service to another group of customers. The cost of providing electricity to rural customers, who are far from the generator and far from each other, is higher than the cost for urban customers.

J. M. Clark recommends discriminatory pricing in *Studies in the Economics of Overhead Costs* (1923),[2] as a solution to the problem of monopoly pricing. This solution is a pragmatic one which recognizes (1) the existence of different costs for different units of business, (2) the social desirability of marginal cost pricing, and (3) the political necessity of a "fair return" price level.

He suggests that the customers of a monopoly be divided into various classes, according to their costs, type of operation, demand, income or other characteristics. Each class should then be treated as a unit of business.

Each unit of business should pay the marginal costs directly traceable to it. Here marginal cost includes expenditures on plant and equipment as well as on variable items. For example, the cost of running power lines to rural users is part of the marginal cost of their service. When service to rural users is added, the cost of rural lines is added.

Thus far, Clark's scheme differs little from the marginal cost pricing scheme; and it confronts the same problem: if price is set equal to the marginal cost of serving each unit of business, will total revenue equal, exceed, or fall below total cost? Clark argues that, most of the time, costs will exceed revenue so that, most of the time, marginal cost pricing leads to bankruptcy. Electric power plants, railroads, pipelines, and most other enterprises are built to meet their peak demand. They are typically built with sufficient capacity to handle all foreseeable customers. Demand is typically below capacity, defined as the minimum point on the average cost curve. Thus, the demand curve typically cuts the marginal cost curve below the average cost curve. Residual costs are not covered by marginal cost pricing.

Clark recommends that residual costs be covered by charging

[2] J. M. Clark, *Studies in the Economics of Overhead Costs* (Chicago: University of Chicago Press, 1923), pp. 175–215, 318–334.

higher prices to some, though not to all, customers. This is price discrimination. Customers are charged different prices for essentially the same service. But, who is to be discriminated against? How is the residual overhead to be allocated?

There are many ways to allocate this overhead among the various classes of customers. All too often, regulatory commissions permit companies to "charge what the traffic will bear." In other words, residual cost is allocated according to differences in the elasticity of demand of different classes of customers. For example, if an electric power company faces competition in the area of home heating, but not in the area of home lighting, it may be allowed to give special low rates to customers who install electric heating and to charge higher rates to other customers. Any relation between this method and the method which is best for society is accidental. The same can be said for various accounting rules-of-thumb which are used to allocate the residual overhead.

Clark prescribes four rules.[3] (1) Residual costs can be allocated according to *ability to pay*. The distinction between "first class" and "tourist class" passengers on airlines is a distinction in ability (and willingness) to pay. (2) Customers who are *causally responsible* for the construction of capacity might be charged all the costs incurred in construction. If a coal mine in an isolated town wants to be connected to the main line of a railroad, the railroad could charge it at a rate which covers all the costs of construction. All of the costs could be treated as the marginal costs traceable to the coal mine. (3) However, other users may *benefit* from the capacity which was built for the coal mine. For example, the people in the town may benefit. Where other users benefit, they might be required to pay something toward overhead. (4) Overhead might be allocated in order to stimulate a greater *utilization of capacity,* as night telephone calls are made at lower rates than day calls.

Clark's list might be expanded to include special rates to stimulate economic growth or technological innovation, or to include special rates based on noneconomic factors. Museums, schools, and military installations might be given low rates. The facts of the case indicate which method should be used, though some cases could call for two or more methods. It is important for any regulatory

[3] *Ibid.,* p. 32.

commission to remember that the rates it sets can improve or damage the operation of the economy.

Clark's scheme for discriminatory pricing and Pigou's scheme for paying bounties have the same goal, the maximum material welfare of society. In Pigou's case, the state collects taxes which it then pays out in bounties. Supposedly, taxes would be collected according to rules that are similar to Clark's rules for allocating residual costs. In Clark's case the regulatory commission permits the monopoly to collect its own bounties.

The promotion of competition

Relatively few markets are natural monopolies. Many markets are such that substantial competition could exist, even if it does not exist. Competition can be reduced by government regulation. It can also be reduced by private manipulation. At the turn of the twentieth century, many industries that had previously been highly competitive were transformed into monopolies or near-monopolies by financial consolidation, by conspiracy, or by predatory tactics.

Antitrust legislation outlaws such anticompetitive activity and, thereby, promotes competition. The Sherman Antitrust Act (1890) was the first major piece of antitrust legislation passed in the United States. It states in broad terms that conspiracy in restraint of trade and monopolization are illegal. The Clayton Antitrust Act (1914) is more detailed. It is directed against specific abusive practices that Congress and President Wilson sought to condemn. Both the Sherman and the Clayton Acts have been amended several times since their passage.

The Sherman Act has two principal sections. Section 1 outlaws conspiracies and combinations which restrict competition. When businessmen get together to fix prices, pool profits, divide markets, or form group boycotts, they are violating the law, and, if convicted, they can be fined and sent to jail. More subtle forms of conspiracy are also illegal. If the activities of trade associations or joint ventures restrict competition, the Attorney General can bring charges against them. If the holder of a legal patent monopoly tries to extend his monopoly by entering into restrictive licensing agreements with competitors, he is violating the law and can be convicted.

Section 2 of the Sherman Act forbids the attempt to monopolize as well as the existence of monopoly itself, except in a few special cases. Companies that attempt to monopolize an industry can be convicted, even if they fail. Companies that actually do monopolize an industry, or become so large that they dominate an industry, can be broken up into smaller more competitive parts, as the old Standard Oil Trust and the old American Tobacco Trust were broken up in 1911.

The Clayton Act was designed to prevent the formation of new monopolies rather than to break up existing monopolies. It was directed against a number of sharp practices that powerful companies had developed to enhance their power. It forbids *exclusive dealing* ("If you buy from me, you can't buy from anyone else.") and *tying contracts* ("If you buy this, you must also buy that.") The American Can Company and Continental Can Company used these devices to restrict competition for many years. They held legal monopoly patents on can-making and can-closing machinery which they leased at low rentals. If a canner wanted to close his cans in the most efficient manner possible, he would have to rent can-closing machinery from American or Continental. In order to rent the machinery, he had to agree to use the cans supplied by the can company and to use no one else's cans. In 1950 the District Court ordered American and Continental to cease these and other restrictive practices.[4]

The Clayton Act also prohibits *price discrimination* (charging different customers different prices for the same type of good where there is no difference in cost) where the effect is to lessen competition substantially. This part of the law makes it illegal for a large company to beat down the price of suppliers and gain a monopoly advantage which is not available to small companies. It also limits local price cutting by giant companies which might try to bankrupt or discipline smaller companies. The Morton Salt Company was convicted under this section of the Clayton Act, as amended by the Robinson-Patman Act, for giving large purchasers excessively large "quantity discounts." The discounts were so large that small grocers complained that they could buy salt for less in neighboring chain

[4] For a more detailed report and analysis of this case see Charles H. Hession, "The Metal Container Industry," in Walter Adams, ed., *The Structure of American Industry* (New York: Macmillan, 1961).

stores at retail than they could buy it from Morton Salt at whole-sale.[5]

One of the most forceful and effective antimonopoly provisions of the Clayton Act is contained in the Celler-Kefauver amendment (1950). The Celler-Kefauver Act, or *Anti-Merger Act,* permits the courts to stop the merging of competing businesses. Under the Sherman Act a company would have to approach the size of a monopoly before the courts could act. By that time, much damage could already have been done. The Celler-Kefauver Act prevents the formation of potential monopolies.

The antitrust laws are based on the hypothesis that competitive markets are more socially desirable than monopolistic markets. They assume that a competitive market structure leads to competitive market performance (no excess capacity, no excess profits, and maximum social welfare). While an empirical proof of this hypothesis would be extremely difficult, there are certainly many individual cases which support it.

[5] Federal Trade Commission v. Morton Salt Company: 334 U.S. 37 (1948).

6

Monopolistic Competition

Criticism of the theories of pure competition and pure monopoly led to the formulation of a more general and more realistic theory. One of the most important advances was made by E. H. Chamberlin in *The Theory of Monopolistic Competition* (1933),[1] on which the present chapter is based. Chamberlin takes the view that pure competition is at one end of the range of all possible market structures. Pure monopoly is at the other end. Monopolistic competition and oligopoly are between these extremes.

Monopolistic competition is one step removed from pure competition. The monopolistically competitive market is similar to the purely competitive market, in that both have large numbers of producers and both have freedom of entry. There are so many producers that they pursue their individual self-interest and do not recognize their mutual interdependence. Monopolistically competitive markets differ from purely competitive markets, in that the former have *differentiated products* and the latter have homogeneous products. Under monopolistic competition each producer

[1] E. H. Chamberlin, *The Theory of Monopolistic Competition* (Cambridge, Mass.: Harvard University Press, 1956), originally published in 1933.

sells a different variety of a general class of products. Each producer has a degree of monopoly control over his product, but he
must face substantial competition from a group of close substitutes.

The market for apartments in a large city is monopolistically
competitive. First, landlords are too numerous and too small for any
of them to have much influence on the market. If one apartment
house were operated rent free, it would hardly affect the rent structure of the city. One landlord does not worry about the rent charged
by one of his competitors. Second, the product of each landlord is
different. If nothing else, the address is different. More likely, the
size, color, and layout of the rooms are different. In the absence of
government regulation, each landlord is free to charge whatever
rent he pleases, though he may not find many tenants at that rent.
He faces competitors, both close and remote.

Product differentiation adds two dimensions to the equilibrium
adjustment. There is not only an equilibrium price and output but
also an equilibrium *product specification* and *sales effort*. The differentiation of the product itself is a matter which the firm must decide. The firm must specify the size, color, quality, location, and
material of its product. In addition, the differentiation of the product makes advertising possible. Through its sales effort, the firm can
attract additional customers. If the product were homogeneous, customers could not tell the product of one firm from another and it
would not pay to advertise.

The following equilibrium analysis is divided into three parts.
First, the equilibrium price and output is discussed. This section, in
turn, is made up of two parts: (1) the equilibrium of the individual
firm and (2) the equilibrium of the group or market. Second, the
equilibrium level of sales effort is examined. Third, the rule which
the profit-maximizing firm uses to differentiate its product is explored.

The Price Decision

Firms must decide the price at which they will sell their product.
Once price is set, the level of output is also determined because the
demand curve shows how much will be sold at each price. How-

ever, since changes in the sales effort and the specification of the product can shift the demand curve, it is necessary to assume that these variables are temporarily constant. The price decision, the sales effort decision, and the product specification decision are actually made at the same time, but, for the sake of exposition, they are treated one at a time.

Individual equilibrium

Two additional assumptions are needed to isolate the price-setting decision of the individual firm. First, the prices of its competitors are assumed to be temporarily constant. As was noted earlier, if the price of one good changes, the quantity demanded of a substitute good will change. If the price of white bread falls, the demand curve for rye bread will shift to the left. Second, the number of competitors is assumed to be constant. Since the market demand for a group of products is given, a doubling of the number or firms will split the market into twice as many parts. The demand curve of an individual firm shifts to the left as new firms enter a market. These two assumptions are removed when the group equilibrium is considered.

The demand curve for the individual firm is downward sloping. See Figure 6-1. Some of its customers are willing to pay more for its product than they are willing to pay for its competitors' products. Perhaps its product is superior, perhaps some customers only think it is, perhaps its product just suits their fancy. Whatever the reason, it is able to sell a few units at high prices, more at moderate prices, and still more at low prices. The demand for its product follows the law of demand.

The marginal revenue curve of the individual firm is below its demand curve, the same as in the case of monopoly. The firm must lower price on all the units it sells, in order to sell one more unit. It gains revenue on the additional unit it sells, but it loses revenue on the previous units it was selling. Thus, the marginal revenue received from selling one more unit is less than the price at which that last unit sells.

The gap between the demand curve and the marginal revenue curve is determined by the price elasticity of demand. When demand is elastic, a small percentage reduction in price produces a larger percentage increase in quantity. The revenue lost because of the lower price is more than made up on the larger volume. When demand is inelastic, the percentage fall in price outweighs the percentage increase in quantity. Total revenue is reduced, and marginal revenue is negative.

Production costs behave the same under monopolistic competition as they do under pure competition. In the short run, every plant must eventually face diminishing returns because it is impossible to increase output indefinitely when at least one input is fixed. The short-run average production cost curve is assumed to be U-shaped and is cut by the marginal production cost curve at its minimum point. Under monopolistic competition it is necessary to refer to average *production* cost (APC) and marginal *production* cost (MPC) since there are also selling costs. For the moment, selling costs are assumed to be zero. In the long run, it is customary, though not necessary, to assume that every firm first encounters internal economies and then internal diseconomies as the scale of its plant is increased. The long-run average production cost curve is also assumed to be U-shaped. The production costs graphed in Figure 6-1 represent either the short run or the long run.

The individual firm is in equilibrium when it is maximizing its profits (or minimizing its losses). Like the competitive firm and the monopoly firm it produces at the point where marginal revenue equals marginal production cost. As long as the addition to revenue exceeds the addition to cost, profits are increased by increasing output. If marginal production cost exceeds marginal revenue, output is too large and should be cut back. The equilibrium output in Figure 6-1 is Q_1.

When the firm knows its equilibrium output (Q_1), it also knows its equilibrium price (P_1). The market clears at one price for each quantity offered. The equilibrium price (P_1) is above the marginal cost of production (MPC_1) because the demand curve is above the marginal revenue curve. The gap between price and marginal production cost is related to the price elasticity of demand—the more inelastic the demand, the greater the gap.

The individual equilibrium price (P_1) may be above or below the average production cost (APC_1). In isolation, the individual firm may earn excess profits or run at a loss. In Figure 6-1 the individual firm is making an excess profit equal to the difference between price

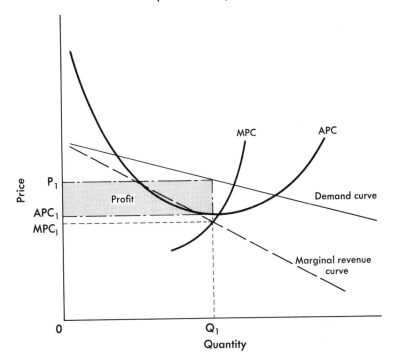

Figure 6-1.
Individual Equilibrium under Monopolistic Competition

(P_1) and average production cost (APC_1) on every unit it sells. It is possible for excess profits (or losses) to exist because it is assumed that competition is temporarily nonexistent. Old firms do not cut price, and new firms do not enter.

Group equilibrium

The equilibrium adjustment for the group occurs when all firms are free to change their individual prices and when all firms are free to enter or leave the industry. Every individual firm will set a price so that its profits are maximized. If excess profits are earned, new firms will enter the industry and, if losses are incurred, old firms will leave the industry.

The entry of new firms divides the market into more parts and reduces the demand for every firm's particular product. Since costs remain unchanged, the fall in demand reduces profits. The inflow of new firms stops when profits are no higher than what can be earned elsewhere. In a similar manner, losses force firms out of business and increase the market share of the remaining firms. The exodus comes to an end when the losses come to an end.

The graph of the group equilibrium adjustment (Figure 6-2) is drawn on the basis of the "heroic assumption" that every firm in the group has identical cost and demand curves. Equilibrium of the group can then be explained by reference to any one firm. This assumption is dropped later. In addition, the marginal cost and revenue curves are omitted from Figure 6-2, for the sake of simplicity.

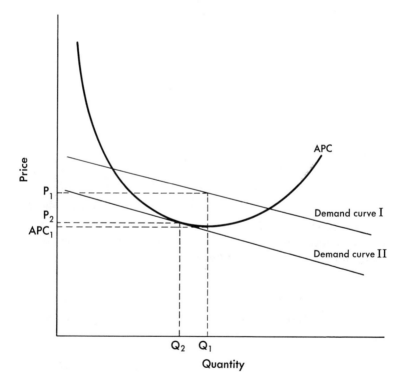

Figure 6-2.
Group Equilibrium under Monopolistic Competition

When the firm in Figure 6-2 faces Demand Curve I, it makes excess profits. Its price (P_1) is above the average cost of production (APC_1). These excess profits induce new firms to enter the industry. The entry of new firms splits the market demand into more parts, and the demand curve facing the individual firm shifts to the left. This shifting continues all the way to Demand Curve II, which is *tangent* to the average production cost curve. Since the price (P_2) equals the average production cost (APC_2) at the point of tangency, all costs of production are covered. There are neither excess profits nor losses, there is no tendency for firms to enter or leave the industry, and no firm can increase its profit by changing its price. The group is in equilibrium at the *point of tangency*.

Three things should be noticed about the group equilibrium under monopolistic competition. First, the equilibrium rate of output is below the capacity rate of output, i.e., output is below the minimum point on the short-run average cost curve. There is excess capacity. Second, the equilibrium scale of plant is not the most efficient scale of plant, i.e., the plant is not at the minimum point on the long-run average cost curve. Third, price is above the least cost of the most efficient plant. These propositions are necessarily true, because it is not possible for a downward sloping demand curve to be tangent to the bottom of a U-shaped cost curve.

If the "heroic assumption" that all firms in the group have identical cost and demand curves is removed, the tendency for excess profits to be eliminated is removed. Some firms may make excess profits either because they have lower costs or because they have a larger, less elastic demand than their competitors. However, the average businessman can not make excess profits. If he did, entry would be encouraged and new firms would compete his extra profits away.

The Sales Effort Decision

In monopolistically competitive markets business enterprises compete with sales effort as well as with price. Sales effort may take many forms: radio, television, and newspaper advertisements; salesmanship; free samples; and so on. Sales effort increases the demand for the firm's product. It also increases the firm's costs.

The sales effort of an individual firm is subject to diminishing returns. Expenditures on sales effort are not equally effective on all potential customers. Selling expenditures attract some customers easily but, as the expenditures are steadily increased, fewer and fewer additional customers are persuaded to buy the advertised product. When a single firm advertises in isolation, its selling costs will tend to be highly productive of additional revenue. When all the firms in the group advertise together, the sales effort of every firm is less effective. Part of the sales effort by one firm is cancelled by the sales effort of other firms.

When a whole industry advertises, the sales of the industry will tend to increase. However, the sales effort of the group is also subject to diminishing returns, and to a certain extent the advertising by one group is cancelled by the advertising of other groups. Just as the advertising of Ford is counteracted by the advertising of Chevrolet, the advertising of automobiles is counteracted by the advertising of airlines. In a sense, every product is in competition with every other product since they are all competing for the consumer dollar. Advertising in general, however, may increase the total amount consumers are willing to spend.

How far will advertising be carried? What is the equilibrium level of advertising for the profit-maximizing firm in isolation and in competition with the group?

In order to isolate the sales effort decision of a single firm, it is necessary to assume that a great many things are temporarily constant: the sales effort of all other firms, the prices of all firms, the product specifications of all firms, and the number of firms. Now, how far does the demand curve facing the isolated firm shift to the right as it increases its selling costs? How much does the quantity demanded (at a constant price) increase as sales effort is increased? When this is known, the individual firm can maximize its profits by equating its additional costs with its additional revenue. The additional costs include production costs as well as selling costs since it is necessary to increase production as the quantity demanded increases. The additional revenue (per unit) is equal to the constant price. Thus, the individual firm is in equilibrium when marginal production cost plus marginal selling cost equals the constant price.

The group is in equilibrium when it is not possible for any firm to increase its profits by increasing its sales effort and when it is not possible for any firm to make excess profits by entering the industry. There is a tendency for competitive advertising, like competitive pricing, to eliminate excess profits from monopolistically competitive industries.

The Product Specification Decision

The rule which the businessman follows in deciding on the specifications of his product is the same rule he has been following all along. He applies the principle of opportunity cost. He weighs every possible type of product against all its alternatives and selects the most profitable one.

The equilibrium adjustment of product specifications is analogous to the equilibrium adjustment of the sales effort. When a firm spends more in designing and improving its product, it shifts the demand for its product, but it also increases its costs. The firm is in equilibrium when it maximizes its profits, and it maximizes its profits when the additional revenue it receives as demand shifts out (at a constant price) is equal to the additional costs of styling, development, and production.

This last rule is of considerable significance. It means that business enterprises profit by increasing the variety of goods available.

The Public Welfare and Monopolistic Competition

Private enterprise and public welfare are not always in harmony under monopolistic competition. It should be added, however, that there is no conceivable social system which could surmount all the shortcomings of monopolistic competition. Product differentiation is a fact and product differentiation is the cause of the imperfection. People prefer a wide variety of goods, and a varied product mix is more costly to produce than a standard one.

First, there is no tendency for production to be carried out to capacity or for the most efficient scale of plant to be built. This is a kind of waste and inefficiency. The price that society pays for a good is greater than the minimum cost at which the good can be produced. As long as the demand curve slopes downward it is profitable for firms to restrict output and to hold price above the least-cost point.

However, if an omnipotent power could set profit-seeking to one side, it would not alter the fact that the demand for an individual product might be above or below the capacity of the most efficient scale of plant when price equals the least cost of production. In isolation, the individual demand curve need not intersect the minimum point on the long-run average cost curve. For example, technical conditions might be such that the most efficient sized shipyard would produce ten 100,000-ton ships a month when operating at its least cost point, but demand conditions might be such that ten 100,000-ton ships are not demanded in a year (at the least-cost price).

Second, advertising does two things that affect the public welfare. On the one hand, it provides the public with information about different products. It makes markets more perfect. Nearly everyone must agree that this is desirable. On the other hand, advertising changes consumer preferences. In technical terms, it changes their indifference maps. This may or may not be desirable.

Competitive advertising between similar products may become redundant. It may simply shift demand from one product to another. It may add to social cost without adding an equal benefit. It is sometimes argued that the television programs, newspapers, and magazines sponsored by advertisers are a redeeming public benefit. However, there is no connection between the price people are willing to pay for such entertainment and the price they actually do pay. People pay for television programs when they buy advertised products, but the programs may be too numerous or too few, too expensive or too cheap, too low-brow or too high-brow for their taste. The programs are profitable because advertising is profitable, not because consumer demand for the programs covers their costs. There is no direct market force which tends to adjust production to demand and price to cost.

When advertising changes consumer preferences, it may induce consumers to buy new products which they ultimately prefer over old products. It may even induce people to produce more, so that they can consume more. Since the development of new products and the growth of production are frequently included among the economic virtues of a society, this aspect of advertising can be counted as a virtue.

Third, quite aside from advertising, the profit motive under monopolistic competition brings forth a wide variety of products. Successful product differentiation, the proverbial "better mouse-trap," brings the reward of temporary excess profits. If it is fair to measure the material welfare of a civilization by the variety of products its people consume, then it is fair to praise monopolistic competition on this point.

The most difficult problem in any discussion of public welfare is the problem of measurement. Each social organization of production and each market structure has its advantages and its disadvantages. Economic theory shows what the advantages and disadvantages are, but it cannot weigh the one against another. Abstract theory cannot strike a balance and prove that, as a whole, advertising is bad or that, as a whole, patent monopolies are good. At its best, economic theory points out what factors are relevant and what quantities should be measured.

7

Oligopoly

An oligopoly is a market of only a few sellers, offering either homogeneous or differentiated products. There are so few sellers that they recognize their mutual dependence. The firms are large, relative to the size of the market. If one firm cuts its price or intensifies its advertising, other firms lose a noticeable volume of sales. When one firm acts it must consider how other firms will react.

Many markets are oligopolistic. If a large steel company cuts its price, it will take such a large volume of business away from its rivals that they may be forced to cut prices, too. If the first steel company expects others to meet its lower price, it may never cut its price in the first place. If four gasoline stations are on the same corner and one of them knocks 3¢ a gallon off its price, the other three can hardly ignore him. If they in turn cut their price, they may force other gasoline stations down the road to cut their price. Gasoline price wars, indeed price wars in general, are a characteristic of oligopolies. The fact that all the supermarkets in one town advertise on Wednesdays only or Thursdays only probably indicates that they have recognized their mutual self-interest. No supermarket wants its Wednesday advertisement bettered on Thursday.

Structure, Conduct, Performance[1]

Despite the importance of oligopolistic markets in the United States, the theory of oligopoly is not as refined as the theories of pure competition, monopoly, and monopolistic competition. Markets that are oligopolistic may differ in every way but one—namely, they contain so few sellers that the sellers recognize their mutual interdependence. The automobile, steel, and petroleum refining industries are oligopolistic. Regional beer, bread, and butter markets are oligopolistic. And, local grocery, theatre, and laundry markets are oligopolistic.

Markets are defined in terms of their structure. The *market structure* is the environment in which the firm works. The principal elements of market structure define the competitive conditions which the firm faces. (1) How many sellers are there? (2) How differentiated are the products? (3) Can new competition enter the market easily. The theories of pure competition, monopoly, and monopolistic competition spell out all three of these conditions. Purely competitive markets have "many" sellers, homogeneous products, and free entry. Monopolistic markets have one seller, no competing products, and no entry. Monopolistically competitive markets have "many" sellers, differentiated products, and free entry. The theory of oligopoly specifies the number of sellers as a "few." This is too narrow a base on which to build a theory covering so many different possibilities. If the theory of oligopoly is to be useful, the analyst must fill in the missing elements of market structure.

In addition to the principal elements of market structure, a number of minor elements are occasionally of critical importance. These minor elements include the nature of demand (its elasticity, its cyclical stability, and its rate of growth) and the nature of costs (their rigidity, the proportion of fixed costs, and the rate of technological change). These minor elements can change the performance of an industry as will be seen in the section on administered price.

Once the market structure of an industry is defined, the conduct of the firm can be deduced from it, on the assumption that the firm

[1] For a more thorough discussion of structure, conduct, and performance see Joe S. Bain, *Industrial Organization* (New York: Wiley, 1959).

tries to maximize its profits. The *conduct* of a firm is the policies which it pursues. Pricing policies, advertising policies, styling policies, purchasing and employment policies, research policies, merger policies, all the policies of the firm are its conduct.

To a great extent, structure determines conduct. If a firm faces a large number of close competitors, its pricing policy will be severely limited. If it is a monopolist, it will have more discretion over its price. If a firm sells a standardized product, styling and advertising policies are limited, if not ruled out.

While structure determines conduct, conduct can also influence structure. John D. Rockefeller conducted his business, the Standard Oil Company, in such a way that he gained a monopoly. He bought up critical pipelines, cut off the supplies of some competitors, undercut the price of others, bought out whom he could, and bankrupted the rest. Once he gained a monopoly he changed his conduct. He raised price and made a monopoly income.

Structure determines conduct, and conduct determines performance. The *performance* of a firm or industry is the service it provides society. Does it produce what consumers want? Does it make excessive profits? Does it cause inflation? Does it contribute to unemployment and economic instability? Is it technologically progressive? These are questions of market performance.

The chain of causation runs from structure to conduct to performance, but some of the links in the chain are weak and unreliable. This is particularly true of oligopolistic market structures. The conduct of one dominant individual can often change the performance of a whole industry. One aggressive price cutter can shatter any tendency toward collusive pricing. The following theoretical discussion offers some insights into the operation of oligopolistic markets, but it does not offer a comprehensive analysis of oligopoly.

Agreement on Pricing Policy

Oligopolies generally have agreements on pricing policies, though sometimes agreements break down. Three separate issues are involved here. First, why is an agreement necessary under oligopoly when it is not necessary under pure competition, monopoly, and monopolistic competition? Second, what price is agreed upon? Is it closer to the monopoly price which maximizes profits for the industry or is it closer to the competitive price which eliminates excessive profits entirely? Third, how is the agreement reached? Is it made in the open or behind closed doors? Is it legal or illegal? All of these issues depend, at least in part, upon the market structure of oligopoly.

Why is an agreement necessary?

The pricing policy of oligopolies is influenced by the fact that there are so few sellers that they recognize their interdependence. The pricing policy of one firm can force a change in the pricing policy of other firms. If one firm cuts price, it can force other firms to cut price, too. For this reason, an agreement on pricing policy is necessary.

Oligopolistic agreements on pricing policy tend to make the prices of identical goods identical and the price differential of differentiated goods uniform. In a given area all name-brand gasoline stations tend to sell their "regular" gasoline at the same price. If one station cuts price, they all cut price. In the same area off-brand stations typically sell at a 2¢ or 3¢ discount. The differential between brand and off-brand gasoline tends to remain uniform. If the major brands change their prices, off-brands also change.

The *kinky-demand curve* in Figure 7-1 shows why an agreement on price is necessary.[2] The kinky-demand curve is really composed of two different demand curves. The more horizontal demand curve (dd′) shows the demand for the product of a single firm in an oligopoly, assuming all other firms in the market hold their prices constant. When just one firm changes price, its sales volume changes sharply, because a small change in the price differential between close substitutes causes a large change in the quantities demanded. The dd′-demand curve is the more elastic curve. It is called the *variety* demand curve. The more vertical demand curve (DD′) shows the demand for the product of the same firm, but on the

[2] The theory of the kinky-demand curve was developed by Paul M. Sweezy, "Demand Conditions under Oligopoly," *The Journal of Political Economy* (1939), pp. 568–573. The interpretation given the kinky-demand curve here is more limited than Sweezy's interpretation.

assumption that all firms in the market change price together. When all firms cut price together, no one firm increases its sales at the expense of anyone else in the market. They all increase sales, because the market demand curve is downward-sloping. The DD'-demand curve is the less elastic curve, and it is called the *apportioned market* demand curve.

The two demand curves form a kink where they intersect. The kink changes when either demand curve shifts. The dd'-demand curve shifts up and down when all the firms in the market change prices. The DD'-demand curve shifts in and out, when the number or size of firms in the industry changes, i.e., when the market is

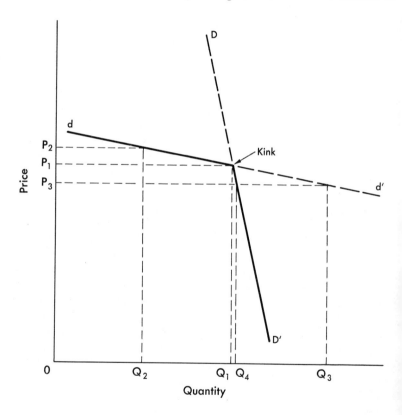

Figure 7-1.
The Kinky-Demand Curve

divided into larger or smaller portions. The two curves may also shift due to changes in consumer incomes, consumer tastes, advertising, or something else.

The equilibrium price is the price at the kink. On the one hand, if a firm raises its price to (P_2) from the equilibrium point (P_1), it will lose sales rapidly (from Q_1 to Q_2). Since the dd'-demand curve is highly elastic, quantity falls relatively more than the price rises. Total revenue declines. Since other firms gain the sales which the first firm loses, it is not in their interest to raise their price. But, since the first firm loses revenue, it is forced to come back down to the equilibrium price (P_1). On the other hand, if one firm lowers its price (to P_3), it gains at first a substantial increase in its sales volume (from Q_1 to Q_3). Total revenue rises. Other firms now lose revenue and are forced to meet the price of the first firm. When all the other firms lower price (to P_3), the first firm has the quantity it sells reduced (from Q_3 to Q_4). The lower price becomes the new equilibrium price, and the variety demand curve (dd') shifts down to that price.

Once the market price has first been set at the kink, ignoring for the moment how it was first set, the firm will lose a substantial volume of sales if it raises its price, and it will force other firms to cut their prices if it lowers its price. Therefore, the actual schedule of quantities which are demanded at various prices traces out the kinky-demand curve, the solid line in Figure 7-1.

The kinky-demand curve is consistent with individual profit maximization. In Figure 7-2 the average cost curve and the marginal cost curve are similar to earlier ones. The kinky-demand curve is the same as the one in Figure 7-1. The upper portion of the marginal revenue corresponds to the dd' portion of the kinky-demand curve, and the lower portion of the marginal revenue curve corresponds to the DD' portion of the kinky-demand curve. Between the two portions of the marginal revenue curve appears a discontinuous gap. When marginal cost passes through this discontinuous gap, the firm maximizes its profits by charging the price at the kink (P_1). If it charges a higher price, marginal revenue exceeds marginal cost. Since the discontinuous gap may be quite large, a large range of different cost structures is consistent with profit maximization at the kink price (P_1). Quite different firms tend to charge the same price.

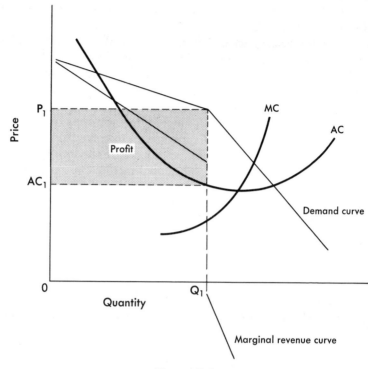

Figure 7-2.
Kinky Demand and Profit Maximization

Does an agreement yield a high or low price?

The kinky-demand curve explains only that an agreement on price is necessary. It does not explain why the kink price is in one place rather than in another. It does not explain whether the price is so high that excessive profits are earned or whether price is so low that losses are incurred. The kinky-demand curve exists merely because there are so few sellers that each one pays attention to both his own and his rivals' prices.

The price level in an oligopolistic market cannot be explained by the sole fact that there are relatively few sellers. More information is needed. In particular, more information is needed about the structure of the market. (1) How few is few? Two or twenty? (2) Is the product differentiated? How differentiated? (3) Is entry easy or difficult?

First, an oligopoly of two or three firms generally behaves differently from an oligopoly of twenty or thirty firms. When there are only a very few firms, the pricing policy of each firm has a great impact on the others. The members of the group are strongly motivated to cooperate and to maximize their joint profits. Because there are only a few firms, it is relatively easy for them to reach an agreement. When there are twenty or more firms in the market, each firm is of less significance. They are not as strongly motivated to act as one. Because there are many firms, it is also difficult for them to reach a mutually beneficial agreement. Price wars occur more frequently in markets of many firms than in markets of a few firms because competition tends to replace cooperation as the number of firms increases.

The size distribution of firms in an industry also affects market behavior. An industry of one hundred producers of equal size is more likely to compete in their pricing policy than an industry of one hundred producers dominated by a "Big Three." If a few firms control a large percentage of the industry output, they can maintain the industry price level by restricting their own output. In addition, they can use various forms of coercion on small companies, so that price cutting is discouraged.

Second, product differentiation gives the individual firm a degree of monopoly power. On the one hand, where goods are homogeneous or standardized, firms are more interdependent than where goods are differentiated. The more homogeneous or the more standardized a group of goods is, the higher is the cross elasticity between goods in the group. If one firm cuts its price, buyers will rapidly substitute its product for rival products. On the other hand, the more differentiated a good is, the more isolated it is from competition. The cross elasticity of demand is low. If a competing firm cuts its price, customers will not readily switch products. The individual firm can, therefore, maintain high prices as rivals cut their prices.

Third, the threat of potential competition can take the place of actual competition. Where it is easy for new firms to enter an industry, it is difficult for old firms to earn excessive profits. Excess profits draw new firms into oligopolistic markets just as excess profits draw firms into purely competitive and monopolistically competitive markets. Not all markets are easy to enter. As Joe Bain points out in *Barriers to New Competition*,[3] there are many advantages which old firms may have that new firms may not.

Economies of scale may block the entry of new firms. If the market is small relative to the most efficient sized plant, established firms may enjoy something like a natural monopoly. The market may be of such a size that two firms can earn excess profits, but a third firm would so expand supply that price would be depressed below the break-even point. Thus, the third firm would never enter and the first two firms would earn monopoly profits indefinitely. Many shopping centers are large enough to support two grocery stores or one hardware store with profits above the competitive level. Yet, if a third grocery store or if a second hardware store entered the same shopping center, the market would be spread too thinly and no one would earn as much as they could get elsewhere.

Established companies may have *absolute cost advantages* over new competitors. The average cost of production may be less for old than for new firms. Old companies may own patents or control natural resources. If new companies enter, they may have to settle for inferior patents, inferior raw materials, or pay royalties to the old companies. This could block the entry of new firms. New firms may have trouble raising capital. Since new ventures are more risky than established operations, owners of capital may ask for higher interest charges or specify more limiting terms on the new than the old. Indeed, potential lenders or investors may find a new venture to be so risky that they ask more than any firm can give. In such a case, entry is blocked.

Product differentiation may be a source of monopoly profits since it is a barrier to entry. If a product is successfully differentiated, it is isolated from the effects of both old and new competition. If a new firm can not attract customers, it can not enter the market. For example, the success and dominance of IBM in the business machine industry is certainly a deterrent to potential entrants. Many companies which may be able to compete on the basis of price and quality do not enter the market because the barrier of customer at-

[3] Joe S. Bain, *Barriers to New Competition* (Cambridge, Mass.: Harvard University Press, 1956).

tachment to IBM is too high. This barrier keeps out potential competitors and allows IBM to make high profits.

How is the agreement reached?

Oligopolies reach agreements on prices in a great many ways. The first and simplest way is by *meeting the price* of competitors, by taking the lowest price in the market. This system (or lack of system) is obviously not favored by businessmen, because it tends to lower profits. It takes only one firm to lower the market price, but all firms must raise price together. Where firms meet the price of their competitors in order to establish uniform prices, price wars are frequent.

Second, when a group of businessmen have competed for many years, they come to know each other very well. Each has a good idea of what the others are thinking. If the union with which they all deal has recently won a large wage increase and if in the past they always raised prices after a wage increase, it is obvious to all that they should raise prices again. No overt or covert price-setting arrangement is needed. They can form a consensus at arm's length. This is called *conscious parallelism* of action or *spontaneous coordination*. Separate companies respond to external forces in similar and mutually beneficial ways.

Price leadership is a third and common way of reaching an agreement on prices. One firm in the industry acts as the price leader. It sets the price and the others follow. The price leader may be the oldest, or the largest, or the most prestigious firm in the industry. The price leader may always be the same, or it may change from time to time. Whatever the case, the other firms respect the price leader's judgment. Price leadership exists in the American steel, cigarette, and petroleum refining industries.

Fourth, the firms in the industry may *collude*. They may meet in a hotel room, they may work through a trade association, they may have interlocking directors, or they may use some other scheme. Collusion is illegal in the United States. In small towns and cities collusion is a common method for reaching agreements. It is rarely discovered, infrequently prosecuted, and almost never convicted. At the local level it is a safe and profitable way of doing business. At the national level the degree of surveillance is greater, indictments are more frequent, conviction is certain, and sometimes the penalty is as great as the ill-gotten gain. Companies of national importance generally avoid so obvious a method of coordinating their pricing policies.

Finally, firms may form a *cartel,* and act as one. A cartel is an organization of many separately owned companies which have a common policy-making agent. The agent typically sets prices and allocates output among the member firms. It may also control styling, advertising, research, and other policies. When an industry is organized into a cartel, or a pool, or a trust, it is no longer an oligopoly, but a monopoly.

The theory of a cartel is virtually the same as the theory of a monopoly. A cartel tries to maximize the joint profits of the industry, though this is not always so easy as it seems, especially where some degree of independence still remains. The price that maximizes the profits of a large and efficient producer may be much lower than the price that maximizes the profits of a smaller firm. Which price will prevail? Will there be a compromise? Even where all firms have the same costs, entrepreneurs may have different opinions on pricing strategy. Some may want high prices and quick returns, while others may prefer low prices to forestall the entry of new competition and yield higher aggregate profits over a longer period of time. Finally, it is frequently not enough to merely set prices and output. Some firms may gain at the expense of other firms in the cartel if they engage in advertising campaigns, develop new products, or introduce cost-reducing methods of production. Thus, the joint profit maximization solution to oligopoly pricing is subject to many limitations.[4]

Administered Prices

Oligopoly prices have often been called *administered prices.* Oligopolists set their own prices. If the demand shifts, an oligopolist may simply change his output, but not his price. In contrast, the

[4] For a careful development of the idea of joint profit maximization see William Fellner, *Competition Among the Few* (New York: Augustus M. Kelley, 1965), original edition published in 1949.

purely competitive firm has no control over the market price. It takes the price which is set in the market, and the market price tends to rise and fall as demand rises and falls.

Administered pricing is one of the areas of great controversy in economic theory and in economic policy. Two major problems which have been blamed on administered prices are inflation and price rigidity. The analysis of these problems is limited here to the way economists use the tools of price theory, though both these problems involve macroeconomic or aggregative issues as well.

Administered prices and inflation

Inflation means a rise in the general level of prices. Three kinds of inflation are distinguished: *demand-pull, cost-push,* and *structural* inflation. As the name indicates, demand-pull inflation occurs when aggregate demand rises relative to aggregate supply. When demand exceeds supply at market prices, prices rise as buyers compete for the limited output. Demand pulls up prices. Demand-pull inflation typically occurs during wartime and during boom times. It is unrelated to administered prices.

Administered prices cause both cost-push and structural inflation. Cost-push inflation occurs when a powerful company or union unilaterally raises its prices (wages) without having to worry about competition. It simply exploits its market power in order to gain a larger income. Whenever American steel companies raise prices or whenever steelworkers gain a wage increase, they are invariably accused of pushing up someone's costs and of pushing up prices in general.

Structural inflation is said to occur because administered prices are flexible upward but inflexible downward. If the composition of demand changes, if, for example, demand shifts from consumer goods to capital goods, the price of capital goods rises, but the price of consumer goods does not fall. Therefore, the average level of prices rises. Structural inflation may also occur over the business cycle. When demand rises, prices rise, but, when demand falls, prices do not fall because of the downward inflexibility of administered prices. Thus, the general level of prices gradually rises.

Inflation, like so many economic phenomena, can be explained in more than one way.

Price rigidity

Oligopoly prices are said to be rigid or inflexible. The rigidity or inflexibility of prices refers to the frequency and amplitude of price changes. When aggregate demand shifts from a depression to a boom or from peacetime to wartime and then shifts back again, the prices of some goods change relatively less than others. In general, manufacturing prices change with less frequency and by a smaller amplitude than agricultural prices. At the same time manufacturing output changes relatively more than agricultural output. In fact, the fall in manufacturing output typically accounts for nearly all the fall in output during depressions. Several quite different theories have been advanced to explain differences in price and output flexibility.

Gardner C. Means,[5] writing in the 1930's, blamed the severity of the Great Depression on the relative inflexibility of administered prices. When demand fell off, the major manufacturing industries maintained their prices, cut back their output, and threw millions of men out of work. At the same time, farm prices fell precipitously while farm output and farm employment were maintained. Farm prices moved down as demand shifted in so that the quantity sold changed little. Thus, Means concluded, if manufacturing had not been concentrated in the hands of a few firms, prices would have been less rigid, and output would have been maintained.

Means' argument is illustrated in Figure 7-3, which stretches reality by presenting manufacturing and agricultural price adjustments on the same graph. Assume that manufacturing and agricultural prices (P_1) were equal in 1929 (at a 1:1 par). Further assume that the demand for both types of products fell to the same level in 1933. Notice that agricultural prices (P_2) are cut by more than half and that agricultural output (Q_2) falls only slightly while manufacturing prices are maintained as output (Q_3) is cut by more than half. Means ascribes this difference in behavior to a difference in monopoly power. Monopolistic manufacturers administer their own prices while competitive farmers take the price as set in the market. Needless to say, many economists dispute this reasoning.

[5] Gardner C. Means, *Industrial Prices and Their Relative Inflexibility*, S. Document 13, 74th Cong., 1st Sess., 1935.

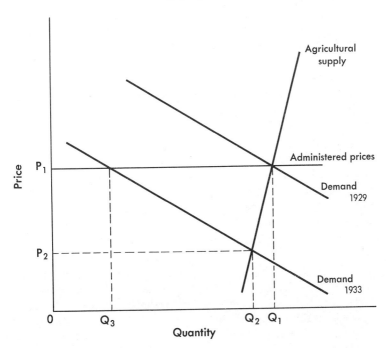

Figure 7-3.
Agricultural versus Manufacturing Price Movements

Paul Sweezy[6] used his kinky-demand curve to explain the rigidity of manufacturing prices. Since much of manufacturing is oligopolistic, the kinky-demand curve applies to manufacturing. It explains why manufacturers with quite different cost conditions find it profitable to charge the kink price. However, it does not explain what happens to the kink price when demand shifts. Therefore, it is not a very strong explanation of the price inflexibility of manufacturing prices during the Great Depression.

Walter F. Crowder and Willard L. Thorp[7] suggest that manu-

[6] Paul Sweezy, "Demand Conditions under Oligopoly," *The Journal of Political Economy* (1939), pp. 568–573.
[7] Willard L. Thorp and Walter F. Crowder, "Concentration and Product Characteristics as Factors in Price-Quantity Behavior," *American Economic Review*, Vol. XL, Supplement (February, 1941), pp. 390–408.

facturing output fell farther than farm output, since many manufactured goods are durable goods, not because manufacturing prices are administered. Since the purchase of new durable goods can be postponed more easily than the purchase of food, the demand for manufactured goods shifted farther to the left than the demand for farm goods. Thus, manufacturing output fell more than farm output. However, this does not explain why agricultural prices fell farther than manufacturing prices.

Alfred C. Neal and Richard Ruggles [8] contend that the relative flexibility of direct cost (average variable cost) determines the relative flexibility of prices. Average variable cost is a floor below which prices cannot fall, because firms will shut down first. However, if input prices fall, average variable costs will fall; and this will permit output prices to fall. Flexible input prices lead to flexible output prices. Cotton textile manufacturers, meat packers, and sugar refiners purchase agricultural products at varying prices, and they sell at varying prices. Automobile, radio, and refrigerator manufacturers have inflexible costs and inflexible prices. A great part of their total costs take the form of wages, either the wages of their own employees or the wages of their suppliers' employees. Since workers resist any attempt to lower their wages, the costs of these manufacturers are not flexible downward. Yet, this does not explain why agricultural prices are flexible in the first place.

J. M. Clark [9] explains differences in price flexibility by differences in fixed costs. On the one hand, in manufacturing, the variable cost is a relatively large percentage of the total cost. When demand falls, a manufacturer may operate far below capacity or even shut down, but he cannot reduce price very far. If he did, he could not meet his payroll. On the other hand, the actual expenditures that a farmer makes in a single year are typically a small portion of his total costs. Land, building, and equipment are purchased only periodically, and much of the cost is the farmer's own "wages." The farmer's income is just what is left over. Price has a long way to fall

[8] Alfred C. Neal, *Industrial Concentration and Price Inflexibility* (Washington: American Council on Public Affairs, 1942), chap. 6; and Richard Ruggles, "The Nature of Price Flexibility and the Determinants of Relative Price Changes in the Economy," *Business Concentration and Price Policy* (Princeton; N.J.: Princeton University Press, 1955), pp. 441–495.
[9] J. M. Clark, *Studies in the Economics of Overhead Costs* (Chicago: University of Chicago Press, 1923), pp. 343–347.

before it reaches the farmers shut-down point. This explains why farmers remain in production as prices fall, but it does not explain why they do not restrict production individually and prevent prices from falling as far as they do. It does not explain MC elasticity.

Alfred Marshall [10] uses the distinction between the market period and the short run to explain differences in price flexibility. If there is a general shift in demand, the temporary impact on agriculture will be quite different from the temporary impact on manufacturing. In agriculture, supply is limited to the stock of goods on hand from harvest to harvest; in manufacturing, it is possible to change output from day to day. In other words, within a year or so, the supply of farm goods tends to be less elastic than the supply of manufactured goods. Therefore, if there is a general fall in demand, farm prices tend to fall farther than manufacturing prices.

Which theory is right? Are they all partly right? What causes the relative inflexibility of manufacturing prices? Theory does not answer this question, but it does point the way for empirical research to find the answer.

Nonprice Competition

While oligopolies are often reluctant to exercise a policy of competitive pricing and prefer a policy of price uniformity and stability, they are not so reluctant to compete with advertising, research and development, location, and other nonprice factors. Nonprice competition is the main force of competition in many industries. There are several reasons why this should be so.

First, price competition is risky and often self-defeating. If a firm cuts price when demand is slack, it may *spoil the market*. When demand increases again, consumers may resist any price increases, or, worse yet, consumers may wait for slack times to buy because they expect price to fall then. In the case of durable goods, fear of spoiling the market is particularly great because the purchase of durable goods can be postponed.

Second, price competition may turn into *cutthroat competition*,

10 Alfred Marshall, *Principles of Economics*, 8th ed. (New York: Macmillan, 1959), pp. 269–291.

especially in an economy which goes through cycles of boom and bust, cycles of deficient and excessive capacity. When there is excess capacity, all the firms can produce more than they are selling. Small price cuts (which expand sales along the dd'-demand curve) appear to be profitable. However, if one firm cuts price, other firms may be forced to follow. If everyone cuts price (given an inelastic DD'-demand curve) everyone will lose revenue. To the isolated individual such price reductions may continue to appear to be profitable, until price has fallen all the way to the shut-down point. To the group such price reductions are frequently destructive.

Third, advertising takes sales away from competitors as does price cutting, but it does not act so quickly and it is not countered so easily as is price cutting. Advertising is most effective over a period of time because it operates on the brand loyalty of consumers. Brand loyalty is a matter of custom and habit. Since custom and habit are not so easily changed as are price quotations, sales effort is a far less aggressive tactic than price cutting. It does not force businessmen to recognize their mutual self-interest as certainly as does price cutting. It is a safer form of competition.

Competition for locations and in research and development are similar to advertising. They are slow acting and are not likely to create an atmosphere of cutthroat competition.

Fourth, some conduct is directed at changing the market structure. Lobbying for tariffs or merging with competitors have the effect of reducing competition. They increase the profits of the individual firm without reducing the profits of the group. They tend to end competition.

Oligopoly and Workable Competition

How well do oligopolistic markets advance the wealth of nations? What standard can be used to evaluate their performance? One standard is pure competition. But pure competition is a difficult standard to apply. Does the American automobile industry perform better in its present oligopolistic form than it would in a purely competitive form? Such a question cannot be answered because the industry's economies of large scale production and differentiation of products make it impossible to establish purely competitive conditions in that industry.

If the strictest meaning of competition is replaced by a more pragmatic meaning, oligopoly may then be evaluated in competitive terms. Many are satisfied with the proposition that the more competitive an industry is, the better its performance is. They are convinced that there is a reliable connection between the structure of an industry (number of producers, barriers to entry, and so on) and the performance of the industry (full employment of resources, least-cost pricing, and so on). They are convinced that the performance of the American automobile industry would be improved if General Motors, Ford, and Chrysler were split up into as many parts as is consistent with today's mass production technology.

A second group of economists is satisfied if an industry is *workably competitive*. They are satisfied if the companies in an industry compete in serving the public and perform satisfactorily. They are satisfied if companies offer the public a wide choice of alternatives at reasonable prices. The industry need not come as close to pure competition as possible. Indeed, they argue that some industries perform more satisfactorily with a noncompetitive market structure. As was mentioned earlier, J. M. Clark believed that a degree of monopoly power is necessary in some industries if they are to avoid destructive competition. J. A. Schumpeter stressed that a degree of monopoly power is necessary to stimulate innovation.

Public policy has taken the advice of both groups from time to time. Government action has weakened competition with laws which restrict agricultural production, patent inventions, and tax imports, but it has strengthened competition with antitrust laws.

8

Supply and Demand in the Factor Market

Why are the rich rich and the poor poor? How is the total income generated from production divided among the members of society? What determines the actual level of wages? or profits? or rent? Why are doctors highly paid and dishwashers poorly paid? Why does land rent for so much in Miami Beach and so little in North Dakota? To a great extent, these things are determined by market forces.

When an individual worker bargains with his employer and when the members of a union bargain with their employer, market forces are present. The relevant range of wages does not run from zero to infinity. Most individuals can work for more than one employer, if they are willing to change jobs, perhaps change residences, or even change occupations. If one employer offers too low a wage, at least some workers will find employment elsewhere. In consequence, the low-wage employer will have trouble staffing his business, and ultimately he may have to raise his wages. Similarly, a union cannot ask for too high a wage and expect to have all its members employed. The employer can substitute machines for men. The employer also can be forced out of business, in which case he would employ no one.

In the past, a number of special theories were used to explain income distribution: a wage theory, a rent theory, a profit theory, and so on.

The *iron law of wages*, derived from the Malthusian population principle, held that wages always tended to be at a subsistence level. Whenever income rose above subsistence, population would increase, divide income into more parts, and force wages back down to subsistence. This kind of theory earned economics the epithet of the "dismal" science.

The doctrine of *Ricardian rent*, developed by David Ricardo in *The Principles of Political Economy and Taxation* (1817),[1] explains the rent of land by the productivity of land. Marginal land on which tenants just break even can bear no rent. If any rent is charged, the tenant farmer will be forced out of business. This is called no-rent land. More productive land does yield a rent which the landlord can claim. The landlord can charge a rent equal to the extra revenue which his land yields above the revenue no-rent land yields. He can collect as rent any excess profits which his tenants may earn due to the superiority of the land. The more productive the land, the higher the rent, and the more the tenant is able to pay.

Today, economists explain the distribution of income with a more general theory—a theory of supply and demand. This theory is much like the theory used to explain prices and output in the product market. The main difference is that business enterprises are now the demanders and consumers or households are the suppliers.

Business enterprises buy inputs in the factor market so they can produce the output which they sell in the product market. The owners of the factors of production sell their services to enterprises so they can buy the products which they consume. The revenue that enterprises receive is the income that factor owners receive. Wages and salaries are distributed to laborers; interest, dividends, and profits go to capitalists; and rent is paid to landlords. The prices that enterprises pay for inputs determines, in part, the cost of pro-

[1] David Ricardo, *The Principles of Political Economy and Taxation* (London: Dent, 1911), originally published in 1817.

duction and thus, in part, determines how much output they supply. The same input prices also determine how much income is distributed to the various factor owners.

The forces that underlie supply differ from the forces that underlie demand in the factor market, as they differ in the product market. The supply of labor and the supply of other productive resources is a matter of individual choice on the part of laborers and other resource owners. The demand for factor services is a *derived demand*. It is derived from the revenue which a factor can earn for a business enterprise.

In this chapter the theory of factor demand will be developed first, then factor supply will be discussed. In the next two chapters, the equilibrium adjustment of supply and demand will be present—first for purely competitive markets and then for monopolized markets.

Factor Demand: The Marginal Productivity Theory

The theory of factor demand is called the *marginal productivity theory*. When the individual businessman is considering buying a new machine, renting extra space, or hiring additional laborers, he asks, "How much revenue will the new unit produce?" "Will it pay for itself?" If the additional (marginal) unit produces more revenue than it costs, it is clearly profitable and is, therefore, demanded. *The extra revenue which marginal units produce determines the demand for them.*

The revenue that an extra unit of land, labor, or capital produces for a firm depends upon two things: (1) how many units the marginal input adds to the firm's output, and (2) how much extra revenue that output brings to the firm. Both of these things have already been discussed in earlier chapters.

The first was discussed in Chapter 3 under the heading, the law of diminishing returns. The law of diminishing returns describes the technical relationship between one input and one output, assuming that at least one other input is fixed. As additional units of an input, say, labor, are taken into production, other inputs remaining constant, output eventually increases at a diminishing rate.

The second—the question of how much the extra output sells for—was discussed in the chapter on consumer demand. Where the demand curve for the product is horizontal, as it is in purely competitive markets, extra output can always be sold at the going price because every firm is so small that it cannot influence the market price. Therefore, marginal revenue equals price. Where the demand curve slopes downward, as it does in monopolized markets, marginal revenue is below price. In order to sell one more unit, the firm must lower price on all the units it sells. The addition to revenue, therefore, is less than the price received on the last unit sold.

The demand curve for labor (or some other factor) shows *how much extra revenue the firm gets from the extra output which an additional laborer produces.* It can be calculated when the technology of the firm and the demand for the output of the firm are known. For example, assume a firm operates with a technology like that in Table 3-1 (repeated in Table 8-1), and assume that the product market is purely competitive with a price and marginal revenue equal to $2.00. The firm's demand for one additional laborer equals the extra output which that laborer produces times $2.00. The whole demand schedule for labor equals the marginal revenue schedule (MR) multiplied by the marginal product schedule (MP). It is called the *marginal revenue product* schedule. MRP = MR × MP.

The marginal revenue product (MRP) curve is the firm's demand curve for labor, because it shows how much labor the firm can profitably hire at various wage rates. At $5.00 a day, the firm will hire eight laborers because the eighth laborer just earns $5.00 for the firm. The eighth laborer adds 2½ units of output (half way between two and three units) [2] which can be sold for $2.00 a unit. If the firm were to hire a ninth laborer, output would rise only 1½ units and revenue would rise only $3.00, so that, at $5.00 a day, the firm would be paying the ninth laborer more than the ninth laborer could earn for the firm. The ninth laborer would reduce profits. If

[2] Where marginal product changes continuously, instead of by discrete steps, marginal product at the point where 8 laborers are employed is 2½, instead of 3. The marginal product of 3 corresponds to the interval bounded by 7 and 8 laborers, and the marginal product of 2 corresponds to the interval bounded by 8 and 9 laborers. Thus, the point at which 8 laborers are employed corresponds to a marginal product of 2½.

fewer than eight laborers were hired, profits could be increased by hiring more labor.

Table 8-1
The Calculation of the Demand for Labor: Pure Competition

Variable Input Labor	Fixed Input Land	Total Product Corn	Marginal Product	Price = Marginal Revenue	Marginal Revenue Product	Value of Marginal Physical Product
0	5	0				
1	5	2	2	$2.00	$ 4.00	$ 4.00
2	5	6	4	2.00	8.00	8.00
3	5	12	6	2.00	12.00	12.00
4	5	19	7	2.00	14.00	14.00
5	5	25	6	2.00	12.00	12.00
6	5	30	5	2.00	10.00	10.00
7	5	34	4	2.00	8.00	8.00
8	5	37	3	2.00	6.00	6.00
9	5	39	2	2.00	4.00	4.00
10	5	40	1	2.00	2.00	2.00
11	5	40½	½	2.00	1.00	1.00

The demand curve for labor (MRP) is graphed in Figure 8-1.[3] It obeys the law of demand and is downward sloping like the demand for products. It slopes downward, because of the law of diminishing returns. The addition to output becomes smaller and smaller as more and more laborers are hired. If only a few laborers are employed, the additional revenue which the last laborer earns for the firm is great, and it is profitable for the firms to pay an additional laborer a high wage. As more and more laborers are employed, the additional revenue which the last laborer earns for the firm falls and the firm will only be willing to hire additional laborers at lower wages.

For example, a farmer who has a crop to be picked will vary

[3] Actually, only the portion of the marginal revenue product curve (MRP) at or below a wage rate of $10 is the demand curve for labor for the same reason that only the portion of the marginal cost curve at or above average variable cost is the supply curve for output. At a higher wage or lower price, the firm will shut down. If, for example, the wage rate were $12 and the firm were to hire 4½ workers (where W = MRP), its total labor cost would be $54 and its total revenue would be $44 (= $2 × 22). Its loss is $10. If it shut down, it would only lose its total fixed cost, or $7.50, where land costs $1.50 an acre.

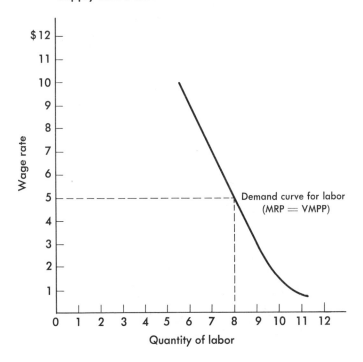

Figure 8-1.
The Demand for Labor under Pure Competition

his instructions to his laborers depending on how much he has to pay them. If labor is expensive, he may send them through his fields or orchards only once, and at a time when most of the crop is ready to be picked, with instructions to pick only what is easily reached. If the price of labor falls, it may be profitable for the farmer to have his workers work over the fields or orchards twice. At a lower wage still, it may pay to send through crew after crew until all the crop is picked including that which is damaged, undersized, or deformed. The quantity of labor demanded rises as the wage of labor falls.

Marginal revenue product (MRP) is distinguished from the value of the marginal physical product (VMPP). The value of the marginal physical product equals market price (P) times marginal physical product (MP). In the case of pure competition, such as that shown in Table 8-1 and Figure 8-1, P = MR, so that VMPP = MRP. In other words, either the VMPP curve or the MRP curve can serve as the demand curve for labor.

In the case of monopoly, the demand curve for the firm's output slopes downward to the right, so that P exceeds MR. Thus, VMPP exceeds MRP. This is shown in Figure 8-2. When the monopolist hires additional laborers to increase his output, he must cut price in order to sell that additional output. To the monopolist the extra output is not worth its price times its quantity, but only its marginal revenue times its quantity. As a result, the additional laborers are only worth their MRP, not their VMPP. For the monopolist, only the MRP curve is the demand curve for labor.

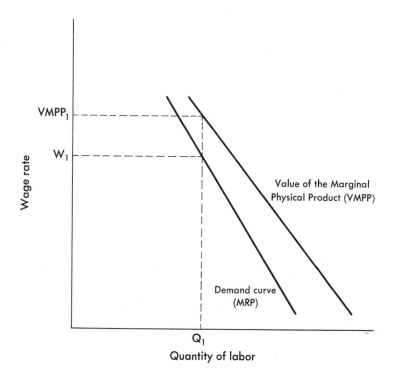

Figure 8-2.
A Monopolist's Demand Curve for Labor

The demand curve for land (or capital) is calculated in the same way that the demand curve for labor is calculated—on the assumption that all other inputs are fixed. As additional units of land are taken into production, output eventually increases at a diminishing rate, i.e., marginal product diminishes. The marginal product of land times marginal revenue equals the marginal revenue product schedule for land, or the demand schedule for land.

Factor Supply

The supply curve for any factor of production shows the quantities that will be supplied at various prices. According to the law of supply, the higher the price is, the greater the quantity supplied. As was mentioned in Chapter 1, every supplier has a price below which he will not sell. This is his reservation price. As price rises, first one, then a few, and eventually many suppliers become willing to sell. In other words, as price rises the quantity supplied rises.

In Figure 8-3, for example, the supply curve for labor slopes upward and to the right because more individual laborers will go to work as the wage rate rises and because individuals will work longer as the wage rate rises. This is why new employers who enter a town sometimes have to pay more than the going wage to attract employees. They must bid workers away from established companies and draw new workers into the market. The same idea applies to land and capital. As towns grow into cities more and more land is demanded, and it is only supplied at higher and higher prices.

Throughout this chapter and the next, it is assumed that market supply curves for all factors slope upward and to the right, though the opposite is possible. One would expect a higher wage to make an hour's work look more attractive and, thus, be an incentive to work longer and harder. However, a higher income means that fewer hours of work are necessary to leave a laborer equally well off. If the effect of the higher income is greater than the effect of the incentive to do more work, the quantity of labor supplied will fall as wages rise. Such a supply curve appears in Figure 8-4, and it is called a *backward bending* supply curve.

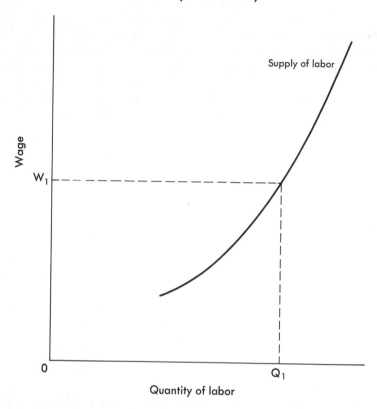

Figure 8-3.
The Supply Curve of Labor

The labor force is not made up of identical men and women, though, to simplify the discussion, this is assumed throughout much of Chapters 9 and 10. The supply of surgeons is not the same as the supply of stevedores. Each worker has his own preferences and abilities while each occupation has its own advantages and requirements. The supply of labor for any occupation is influenced by the cost of training, the ability of laborers, the preferences of the laborers, and artificial barriers as well as the wage rate.

The cost of training is a barrier that limits the supply of laborers in many occupations. The financial burden of four years of

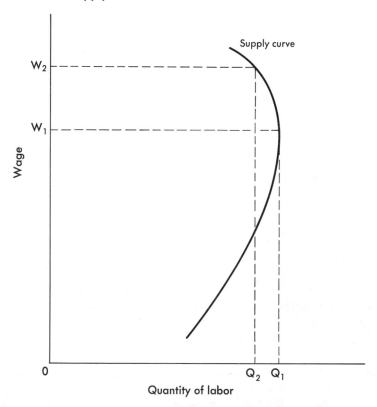

Figure 8-4.
The Backward-Bending Supply Curve

college is frequently too great for low-income families to bear, especially when the alternative is an immediate increase in family income if a child starts to work early. Even when the costs of formal education are not great, the cost of many years of apprenticeship at low wages may restrict the supply of labor. Kitchen help, for example, is notoriously low paid, yet accomplished chefs frequently earn high salaries. Similarly, many of the highest paying positions in the business world can only be filled by men who have nearly a lifetime of experience.

The supply of labor is limited in some occupations because

few laborers have the innate ability to do the job. Intelligence, beauty, strength, and so on are not equally distributed among the population, though they are probably more equally distributed than is income. Not everyone can be a research physicist, an opera singer, or a professional golfer. Similarly, not everyone can be a successful salesman, labor negotiator, or lawyer. For one reason or another, most people are not suited to these occupations.

The supply of labor is limited in many occupations because people find the work to be unpleasant, degrading, or unfamiliar. Dirty jobs, such as coal mining and garbage collecting; dangerous jobs, such as bridge and tunnel construction; and jobs in remote areas, such as the Arctic or the Tropics, typically pay more than the average. Many people will take them only if they are offered higher wages than they can get elsewhere.

In the opposite case, the supply of labor in some occupations is expanded, because the work is stimulating, honorable, or morally uplifting. White-collar jobs are generally preferred over blue-collar jobs because the former are the more respectable in the eyes of society. Bank clerks have earned very low wages for years, preferring instead the honorable status with which that occupation is viewed by the community. Teachers, nurses, and welfare workers are generally poorly paid, not, to be sure, because of the status attached to such occupations, but because of the personal gratification that people find in such work.

Unions and licensure laws as well as discrimination based on race, religion, and sex are artificial barriers that restrict the supply of labor in some occupations and expand the supply of labor in other occupations. As might be expected from the chapter on elementary supply and demand, when supply is restricted, the wage is enhanced, and when supply is expanded, the wage is depressed. In Chapter 9, it is assumed that there are no monopoly restrictions of supply, though there may be other restrictions. In Chapter 10, monopoly restrictions are considered.

9

Pure Competition and the Factor Market

The scarcity of productive resources raises three basic questions. (1) What quantity and what quality of goods will be produced? (2) How will goods be produced? And, (3) for whom will goods be produced?

While all of these questions are closely interrelated, the first has been emphasized in the chapters on the product market. Consumer demand, as measured in prices, is the magnet that attracts different goods in different quantities and qualities. The cost of production and monopoly power are the forces that resist the pull of consumer demand. These forces are in equilibrium when profits are at the maximum that the market structure permits.

The last two questions are emphasized in the analysis of the factor market. The method of production depends partly on the productiveness of alternative resources and partly on their scarcity as reflected in their price. It is technically possible to make most things in a variety of ways and with a variety of materials. Hand-tooled automobiles and solid silver sewer pipes can easily be made. They are surely as good and as serviceable as everyday automobiles and sewer pipes. They involve no technical problems that have not been mastered, and they are made from available resources. However, skilled labor is too expensive to use in the handicraft production of automobiles, and silver is too expensive to use in place of clay or cast iron. Such scarce and high-priced resources cannot profitably be used in such inefficient and unremunerative ways.

The distribution of income among resource owners depends partly on productivity and partly on scarcity. It depends partly on demand and partly on supply. Some absolutely essential resources earn little or no income, because they are so abundant. Few natural resources are more essential than the sun and the air, yet they are free. They receive no part of the output they help produce. Water that was once free and land that was nearly free in the United States now command a price, though there is probably no less water and certainly no less land than there was before. Today they yield a revenue where previously they did not because the demand for them has increased.

Production for a profit is the rule in the factor market as it is in the product market. And, as in the product market, profit maximization produces one equilibrium under competition and another equilibrium under monopoly. The competitive equilibrium is discussed in this chapter, monopoly is discussed in the next chapter.

Pure Competition Defined

Purely competitive markets have so many buyers and sellers that no one of them can alter the equilibrium of supply and demand. The individual transactor takes the price as set in the market. He does not set the price himself. By implication, the product or factor of production must be homogeneous. No material or immaterial distinction can be made between what one trader offers to sell and what another offers. One brick is like other bricks and one bricklayer is like other bricklayers. Finally, anyone can enter the market.

Supply and Demand

The equilibrium price in the factor market is determined by supply and demand. The market supply curve is simply the sum of the supply curves of all individual factor owners, and the market demand curve is simply the sum of the demand curves of all individual enterprises. Supply and demand are conventionally treated as independent forces, though in fact they are not independent, as the circular flow diagram (Figure 0-1) illustrated. The demand for an input depends partly on the price of the output, which in turn depends partly on the income of households, which, following the circular flow, depends partly on the price of the factor. It is possible for an income change in the factor market to cause a demand change in the product market. However, at the elementary level it is best to ignore such complicated repercussions and to assume that the equilibrium adjustment of each market takes place in isolation from the other market.[1]

In the factor market, the market supply curve is upward sloping because individual factor owners tend to sell more of their resource as the price goes up. To the individual competitive firm, however, the supply curve is horizontal. See Figure 9-1. Under pure competition, the individual firm can, for example, hire all the labor it wants at the market wage because it hires only a small part of all the labor in the market. One retail store cannot change the general wage rate for clerks. If it offers less than the going wage, it cannot hire anyone. If it offers more, it is wasting its money. To the firm, the supply curve is perfectly elastic at the ruling market wage.

Since the supply curve is horizontal, the firm can always hire additional laborers at the going wage. The supply curve is, then, the *marginal outlay* curve (MO) because it shows the additional outlay which a firm must make to hire an additional laborer. If the market wage goes up or down, the supply curve to the firm and the marginal outlay curve of the firm will be shifted up or down.

The firm's demand curve for labor is its marginal revenue product (MRP) curve for labor. It is downward sloping because each additional laborer produces a smaller addition to output. The firm can profitably use more laborers at a lower wage than at a higher wage. The quantity of laborers demanded rises as the wage rate falls. The market demand curve in Figure 9-1 is assumed to be made up of 1,000 identical individual firm demand curves.

[1] Under pure competition, the individual marginal revenue product curve is calculated on the assumption that the product price is constant. $MRP = P \times MP$. In Figure 9-1 the market demand curve is drawn on the same assumption, even though product prices probably will change as the output of many companies changes at the same time.

Equilibrium

The individual firm is in equilibrium when it maximizes its profits, and it maximizes its profits where MRP = MO. If the marginal revenue product of labor exceeds the marginal outlay on labor, the firm can increase its profits by hiring more labor. The addition to revenue exceeds the addition to expense. Similarly, if marginal outlay exceeds marginal revenue product, the firm can increase its profits by laying off workers. Costs fall more than revenues until the point where MRP = MO is again reached. In Figure 9-1, the firm maximizes its profits by hiring Q_1 laborers at a wage of W_1.

Remember the rule for profit maximization in the factor market: MRP = MO.

In Figure 9-1, the market is also in equilibrium at wage W_1, the wage that equates the quantity supplied and the quantity demanded. If the wage temporarily rises above this point, say, to W_2, the quantity demanded falls and the quantity supplied rises. More men are willing to work at the higher wage, but businesses employ fewer men. In other words, some men who are willing to work at the higher wage cannot find work. However, since most

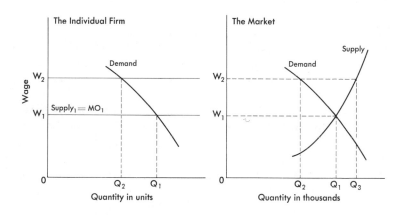

Figure 9-1.
Equilibrium for the Firm and in the Market for Labor

of the laborers would rather work for lower wages than be unemployed, unemployed workers offer to work for less. This tends to bring the wage rate down. As the wage falls toward the equilibrium level, businesses employ more men because more men can profitably be employed at the lower wage. At the same time, fewer men are supplied because some workers will only work at the higher wage. The market is in equilibrium when the quantity demanded equals the quantity supplied.

What is true for an isolated labor market is not necessarily true for all labor markets together. While a cut in wages will eliminate unemployment in an isolated market, such as the market for fruit pickers in California, a cut in wages will not necessarily eliminate nationwide unemployment, because such a widespread cut in wages would surely reduce consumer incomes, thereby reducing product demand, and finally, reducing the demand for labor itself.

If wages were temporarily to fall below the equilibrium level, the quantity demanded would exceed the quantity supplied. As wages fell, more and more laborers would refuse to work at the same time that businessmen would find it profitable to hire more and more laborers. The quantity demanded would exceed the quantity supplied, and there would be a labor shortage. The businesses that offered the highest wages would get the available supply. Thus, the wage would tend to rise and to bring the quantity demanded into equilibrium with the quantity supplied. In equilibrium, those workers who are willing to work at or below the market wage are employed and those employers who are willing to pay a wage equal to or greater than the market wage for every worker hired do the employing.

In equilibrium, all workers are paid a wage equal to the marginal revenue product of the last laborer employed. This is necessarily true if the market is purely competitive ($MO = W$) and if businessmen maximize their profits ($MRP = MO$). Thus, $MRP = MO = W$.

Long-Run Tendencies

In the long run, natural and human resources tend to move into those places and uses where the rewards are the greatest and tend to move out of those places and uses where the rewards are the least. Excess profits tend to be eliminated by the entry of new firms, and losses tend to be eliminated by the exit of firms. Regional wage differentials tend to be eliminated by the movement of labor into high-wage areas and out of low-wage areas. Different kinds of labor tend to be paid wages in proportion to their productivity, land tends to earn a rent in proportion to the productivity of the land, and capital tends to yield an interest in proportion to the output attributable to capital.

These long-run tendencies are the equilibrium to which existing market forces are pointing. The long run is never actually reached because fresh changes are always disturbing the existing market forces. If excess profits exist today in the hat industry, new firms will certainly tend to enter the industry and eliminate those excess profits. However, if hats go out of fashion tomorrow, losses may suddenly appear in the industry. The new long-run tendency is for firms to go out of business. Some of these long-run tendencies need to be explored with more care.

In the factor market, the demand for factors tends to shift to the right, when excess profits induce new firms to enter the industry, because the new firms must buy resources in order to operate. If an industry purchases a significant portion of some factors, the price of those factors will tend to rise as new firms enter the industry. The rise in factor prices tends to eliminate excess profits just as the fall in product prices tends to eliminate excess profits. Where losses exist, the exit of firms shifts factor demand to the left. This tends to reduce factor prices and to wipe out the losses.

To illustrate, one of the consequences of the farm program in the United States has been a rise in the price of farm land. When the government restricts farm production and purchases farm products in order to raise the income of farmers, it also raises the price of farm land. Because farming is made more profitable by the programs, each farmer acting in his own self-interest tries to buy more land. As farmers bid against each other, the price of land goes up. Those farmers who had land to start with have enjoyed a sizeable appreciation of their assets. Those who buy land at the higher prices will only earn the competitive rate of return on their investment.

The profit motive which causes firms to enter or leave an industry also tends to shift resources from one industry to another. When automobiles were first replacing buggies, the increase in the size and the number of automobile companies increased the demand for auto mechanics while the decrease in the size and the number of buggy companies decreased the demand for wheelwrights, harness makers, and so on. The rise in the demand for mechanics tended to increase the wage of mechanics while the fall in demand for wheelwrights tended to decrease the wage of wheelwrights. The rising wage of mechanics attracted workers into the automobile industry while the falling wage of wheelwrights repelled men from the buggy industry.

In a similar way, the market tends to eliminate regional wage differentials. For example, for over a century in the United States, wages have been significantly higher in the North than in the South. In response, workers have tended to move North, particularly Negroes and other poorly paid workers. Industry has tended to move South, especially those industries that used a great deal of labor, like the textile industry which once flourished in New England. The migration of companies and workers has tended to reduce the North-South wage differential, as the per capita income data in Table 9-1 illustrate. In 1930, per capita income in the Southeast was 39% of that in New England. By 1960, per capita income in the Southeast had risen to 65% of that in New England.

Table 9-1
The North-South Differential in Per Capita Income *

Region	1930	1940	1950	1960
Southeast	$313	$343	$1,009	$1,601
New England	806	757	1,628	2,466
Southeast/New England	39%	45%	62%	65%

* Office of Business Economics, *U.S. Income and Output* and *Survey of Current Business* (April 1964), p. 18. The percentages were calculated by the author.

Simple supply and demand curves can be used to show how the migration of workers and companies has tended to eliminate the North-South wage differential. The supply and demand curves on the left in Figure 9-2 are for the North and those on the right are for the South. When workers leave the South for the higher wages in the North, the supply curve for labor in the South shifts

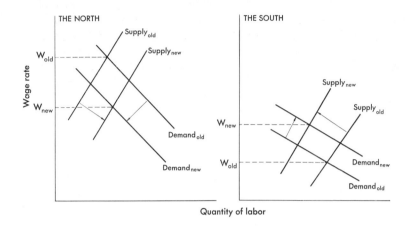

Figure 9-2.
The North-South Wage Differential

to the left and the supply curve for labor in the North shifts to the right. Similarly, when companies leave the North for the South, the demand for labor falls in the North and rises in the South. The wage in the South rises while the wage in the North falls. To be more factual, the wage in the South rises relative to the wage in the North.

In the long run, each factor of production is paid for in proportion to its productivity. If greater profits can be earned using one factor of production (capital) than can be earned using another factor of production (labor), businesses will tend to use more capital and less labor. The substitution of capital for labor tends to bring the rate of return of each factor into proportion to its productivity. As firms use more and more capital, the marginal revenue product of capital diminishes. As firms simultaneously use less and less labor, the marginal revenue product of labor rises. The firm maximizes its profits when the last dollar spent on capital generates the same amount of revenue as the last dollar spent on labor. If the last dollar spent on capital produced more than the last dollar spent on labor, clearly more should be spent on capital and less on labor.

In equilibrium, two conditions hold. First, each factor of production earns a rate of return equal to its marginal revenue product.

$$\text{Wages} = \text{MRP}_{\text{labor}}$$
$$\text{Rent} = \text{MRP}_{\text{land}}$$
$$\text{Interest} = \text{MRP}_{\text{capital}}$$

If the MRP of labor exceeded the wage of labor, the firm could increase its profits by hiring more labor. The addition to revenue would exceed the addition to expenditures. As more laborers are hired, the MRP of labor falls. The firm maximizes its profits where the MRP of labor equals the MO of labor equals the wage of labor. The same principle applies to all factors of production.

Since under pure competition MRP = VMPP, each factor of production is also paid an amount equal to the market value of the physical output of the marginal unit. If the last automobile assembly worker increases output by 2 cars a year and the cars sell for $2,500 each, he and all similar workers will be paid $5,000 a year.

Second, the rate of interest relative to the marginal revenue product of capital equals the rate of wages relative to the marginal revenue product of labor, and they equal the rent of land relative to the marginal revenue product of land. This is the *proportion of factors rule:*

$$\frac{\text{Interest}}{\text{MRP}_{\text{capital}}} = \frac{\text{Wage}}{\text{MRP}_{\text{labor}}} = \frac{\text{Rent}}{\text{MRP}_{\text{land}}}$$

The last dollar of interest generates the same amount of revenue as the last dollar of wages or the last dollar of rent. This is the rule the firm follows to minimize its cost of producing any given output. If the marginal mechanic is more productive than the marginal car washer, mechanics are paid more than car washers in proportion to their respective productivities. The firm gets the most it can from every dollar it spends.

Moral, Political, and Scientific Views

What does the marginal productivity theory of income distribution under pure competition mean? Does it mean that income is fairly and equitably distributed under competitive market conditions? Does it mean that income is distributed in such a way that social welfare is maximized? Or, does it merely mean that income is distributed according to physical productiveness and nothing more?

Whether income is "fairly and equitably" distributed is a question of moral philosophy. The famous American economist, J. B. Clark, argues in his *The Distribution of Wealth* (1899) that competitive markets do distribute income fairly and equitably.[2] His reasoning is as follows:

Ethical proposition: every man should be paid according to the rule, "To each what he creates." This simple, just, and natural law is the moral basis of private property. Any society that does not follow this rule is a society that condones institutional robbery.

Theoretical proposition: under pure competition the rate of return to each factor equals the value of the marginal output of that factor (VMPP). The output attributable to the last (marginal) laborer employed determines the wage of labor. The same is true for the rent of land and the interest on capital. If all land is alike, if all capital is alike, and if all labor is alike, any particular unit of a factor can be treated as the marginal unit. If one laborer is withdrawn from production, output will fall by the same amount it would fall if any other laborer had been withdrawn from production. The profit maximizing businessman can just afford to pay the last laborer the value of his marginal product; and, since all laborers are alike, all laborers are paid a wage equal to that of the marginal laborer. If all laborers are not alike, they will be paid according to their individual productiveness.

Conclusion: since any laborer can be treated as the marginal laborer and since the marginal laborer receives the value of what he creates, labor in general receives what it creates. By the same reasoning, the owners of land and the owners of capital receive what their factor services create. Thus, the market is in harmony with the laws of nature.

J. B. Clark's philosophy can be criticized on many points. Most obvious, his rule, "To each what he creates," can be replaced by the socialist rule, "From each according to his ability, to each according

2 J. B. Clark, *The Distribution of Wealth* (New York: Kelley and Millman, 1956), originally published in 1899. J. B. Clark was the father of J. M. Clark, referred to earlier.

to his need." The question of which rule is better is a question of ethics and it can not be answered by economic theory. What is not so obvious is that J. B. Clark does not inquire into how property owners got their property in the first place. Certainly many land-lords and capitalists received their property by inheritance and not by any production of their own. Thus, by Clark's own rule, they receive what they did not create, and they are the agents of institutional robbery.

One level removed from the moral philosophy of J. B. Clark is the welfare economics of A. C. Pigou.[3] Pigou does not discuss the morality of production for a profit under pure competition; rather, he wants to know whether the private enterprise system maximizes social welfare and, if it does not, what action by the state can. He is a political economist. His reasoning in an abbreviated form proceeds along the following line:

Value judgment: social welfare is, in general, at a maximum when physical output is at a maximum, assuming people are not forced to work and assuming welfare could not be increased by redistributing existing output, income, and wealth.

Welfare proposition: the total output for society is at a maximum when the *marginal social product* of each factor of production is equal in all its alternative uses. The marginal social product is the extra output that accrues to society when a marginal factor is employed. If the marginal social product of labor were greater in the North than in the South or if it were greater in the automobile industry than in agriculture, then total output could be increased by shifting laborers from the South to the North and from farming to making automobiles. As long as a laborer can produce more for society in one place than another, output can be increased by putting him in the place where he produces the most. When the marginal social product of one type of factor is everywhere the same, and the marginal social product of other types of factors is everywhere the same, total output cannot be increased by reallocating resources.

Economic theory proposition: under pure competition the *marginal private product* of each factor of production tends to be the same in all its alternative uses. The marginal private product

---

[3] A. C. Pigou, *The Economics of Welfare* (London: Macmillan, 1960), first printed in 1920.

of a factor of production is the extra output attributable to that factor which also accrues to that factor. It is the VMPP of each factor, which under pure competition equals the MRP of each factor and also equals the rate of return to each factor.

The marginal private product of labor tends to equal the wage of labor, the marginal private product of land tends to equal the rent of land, and the marginal private product of capital tends to equal the interest on capital. If a laborer, landlord, or capitalist could get more income in one place or use than another, he would, as a matter of self-interest, shift his services to the higher-income area. The shifting of resources from low- to high-income areas increases the VMPP and rate of return in low-income areas. In equilibrium, the VMPP of each factor is the same in all its alternative uses, and the rate of return to each type of input is everywhere the same, assuming that resources are perfectly free to move, that the owners of resources know about their alternatives, and that there are no elements of monopoly to restrict the flow of resources.

Political conclusion: if the marginal product for society equals the marginal product for the individual, then the self-seeking of individuals under the rule of competition will maximize social welfare. The government should pursue a policy of *laissez-faire*. Where marginal social products do not equal marginal private products, the government should act to equate them.

If steel companies pollute rivers and the air and thus inflict costs on society which they do not pay, the state should require them to purify their smoke and treat their sewage. If monopolies restrict the flow of resources, they should either be broken up or regulated. If inventors do not receive compensation for their efforts, the government should grant them patents of monopoly. In short, A. C. Pigou concludes that the private enterprise system can maximize material welfare, but that state intervention is sometimes necessary to assure that it does.

The scientific view of the marginal productivity theory under pure competition does not consider the theory a moral justification for private property or a political justification for either state action or inaction. It considers the theory as an explanation of how such markets function and as a tool to analyze the impact that disturbing forces might have on the allocation of resources and the distribution of income. The mechanics of the theory are the same according to all three views: the moral, the political, and the scientific. The three views differ only in their interpretation and use of the theory.

The scientific view sticks to the mechanics of the theory. Under pure competition a factor of production is paid according to the productivity of the last unit of that factor taken into production. If the factor is scarce, relative to the demand for it (e.g., high-grade gold-bearing land), it will yield a relatively high income. If a factor is abundant, relative to the demand for it (e.g., common labor), it will earn relatively little. No-hit pitchers, popular singers, and top executives earn high salaries because they are relatively scarce; clergymen, symphony composers, and migratory farm laborers earn low incomes because they are numerous relative to the demand for them.

Under pure competition, the market assigns a high price to relatively scarce factors and a low price to relatively abundant factors. This encourages the use of abundant factors as it discourages the use of scarce factors. If the government subsidizes the education of doctors or lawyers, they will become more abundant and their incomes will fall. If the government restricts the production of cotton, the income of cotton farmers will rise. Whether government intervention is socially, morally, or politically desirable is not a scientific question.

10

Monopoly Power and the Factor Market

Monopoly power exists whenever a single transactor or united group of transactors have the power to alter the market price. If a baseball player, top executive, or popular singer has the power to raise his wages by threatening to quit, he has monopoly power. If a union has the power to raise wages by threatening to strike, it has monopoly power. If a company has the power to lower wages by laying off workers, it has monopoly power.

Monopoly power can enter the factor market from several sides. First, the owners of resources have monopoly power if they can restrict the total supply of their type of resource. Such monopoly power can earn a monopoly income for resource owners. Second, enterprises that purchase resources have monopoly power if they can alter the market price by changing the quantity of resources they buy. This type of monopoly power is called *monopsony* (from the Greek meaning "one buyer"). It can lead to monopsonistic exploitation. Third, monopoly power can enter the factor market from the product market. Where monopoly power in the product market exists, monopolistic exploitation in the factor market occurs. All three types of monopoly power can enter a factor market at the same time, but they will be treated one at a time.

Monopoly Control of Resources

Monopoly control of resources enables resource owners to raise their incomes, because it enables them to restrict supply and raise price. This is illustrated in Figure 10-1. When supply is unrestricted, the price (rate of return to the factor) is determined by the intersection of the supply and demand curves. When supply is restricted, a smaller quantity is offered for sale at every price. The price with

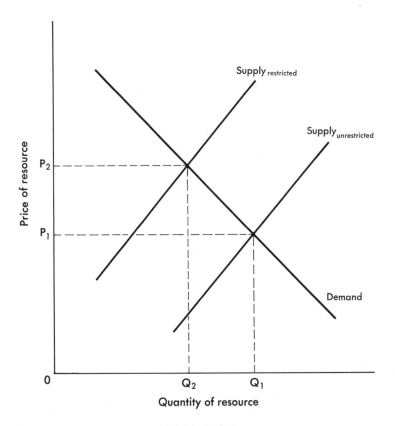

Figure 10-1.
Monopoly Control of a Resource

supply restricted (P_2) is above the price with supply unrestricted (P_1). Because the demand curve is downward sloping, the equilibrium price is higher, when the supply curve is farther to the left.

The market price (rate of return to a factor) tends to rise steadily as supply is restricted, but the total income to the monopolizing individual or group may fall as price rises. The maximum total income depends upon the elasticity of demand. If demand is elastic, the percentage fall in quantity exceeds the percentage rise in price. Thus, where demand is elastic, total income falls as price rises. If demand is inelastic, the percentage rise in price exceeds the percentage fall in quantity, so that total income rises as price rises. Where the demand curve is unitarily elastic, total income for the resource is maximized.[1]

When the monopoly power is held by a group, the leadership of the group may try to maximize the income of those who remain in the group as the quantity demanded falls, instead of maximizing income for everyone. For example, the United Mine Workers under John L. Lewis adopted the policy of getting a decent wage for those miners who work. However, as the wage of coal miners was pushed up, mine operators substituted machines for men and threw men out of work. The size of the union was greatly reduced, but the wages of its members remain among the highest in the country.

The ways in which supply can be restricted are practically endless. Some are obvious, some are not. The restriction of supply is obvious when the Texas Railroad Commission limits the production of crude oil in Texas to one-third of the maximum efficient rate of recovery (MER). The State of Texas and her sister oil states run a cartel for oil producers. They raise the income of oilmen by restricting production and by raising the U.S. price of crude oil far above the world price, which is itself a cartel price.[2] The restriction is equally obvious when all electricians, or plumbers, or steelworkers join together in a union to press for higher wages and better working conditions.

The monopoly restriction is not so obvious if it merely restricts people from entering an occupation. The effect is the same. When

[1] The interrelationship between price, elasticity, and income (total revenue) is discussed more thoroughly in Chapter 2.

[2] For a longer discussion of the petroleum industry see J. B. Dirlam, "The Petroleum Industry," in Walter Adams, ed., *The Structure of American Industry* (New York: Macmillan, 1961), pp. 277–310.

the printers' union requires long apprenticeships, it restricts the supply of printers and raises their wages. When the law requires that medical doctors be licensed, the supply of doctors is restricted in proportion to the difficulty of getting a license; a license becomes very difficult to get when years of specialization follow years of internship after years of medical school preceded by years of college. When universities specify that only Ph.D.'s may become tenured faculty members, they restrict the supply of university teachers and raise their salaries.

The question whether all these restrictions are "good" or "bad" is not at issue here The point here is simply that a restriction of supply will tend to raise the rate of return to factor owners.

Exploitation

The word "exploitation" has an evil connotation. It raises images of poor children working long hours in dark and dusty spinning mills, of coal miners entering mines before sunup, leaving after sundown, and not seeing the sun until Sunday, or of boys, rather than mules, pulling barges along canals because boys are cheaper than mules.

In economics, the word "exploitation" has a technical meaning. Joan Robinson defines exploitation in her *The Economics of Imperfect Competition* in the following way: *laborers are exploited, if their wage is below the value of their marginal physical product (VMPP).*[3] Two conditions can cause a divergence of the wage rate from the value of the marginal physical product of labor: first, monopsonistic power in the factor market; second, monopolistic power in the product market. These conditions give rise to monopsonistic exploitation and monopolistic exploitation, respectively.

Monopsonistic exploitation

A single enterprise can "exploit" a resource when it buys a large portion of the whole resource supply. A large mine operator in a

[3] Joan Robinson, *The Economics of Imperfect Competition* (London: Macmillan, 1954), pp. 281–304; originally published in 1933.

small and isolated town has the power to exploit his workers if he is the principal source of employment in the town. If he dismisses a significant number of workers, he can reduce the wage he has to pay those he does employ. Workers have the choice of working at a lower wage or not working at all. Some workers will not work at the lower wage. They will either retire or move away. However, many workers will prefer to work at the lower wage rather than move or be unemployed.

The resource supply curve facing the monopolist is the market supply curve. It follows the law of supply: the higher the price, the greater the quantity supplied; the lower the price, the smaller the quantity supplied. The monopsonist can lower the wage by laying off workers, yet he must employ workers in order to produce the output he sells in the product market. To produce more output, he must employ more labor; he has to pay a higher wage in order to attract a greater quantity of labor.

The monopsonist must raise his wage to get additional laborers, and, when he raises his wage for new employees, he must also raise the wage for old employees. Let us suppose that he is currently employing 100 workers at a salary of $1.30 an hour and that he wants to hire another 20 workers whom he must pay $1.40 an hour in order to get them to work for him. If he does not also pay his old workers $1.40 an hour, they would quit and reapply for employment at $1.40 an hour. If he wants to employ 120 workers of a given grade, he must pay them all $1.40 an hour. The added expense (marginal outlay) of 20 additional laborers is more than their wage times 20. It is their wage times 20 *plus* the additional 10 cents an hour he must pay his 100 original workers. That is, his marginal outlay is $20 \times \$1.40 + 100 \times \$.10$, which equals a total of $38.00 for 20 new workers, or $1.90 per hour per additional worker.

The marginal outlay (MO) curve for a monopsonist lies above the supply curve. This is shown in Figure 10-2. Each time the monopsonist wants to hire more laborers he must raise wages to both the old and the new workers. Thus, the marginal outlay curve rises more steeply than does the average outlay (supply) curve. Similarly, the monopsonist can lower the wage he pays all his workers by employing fewer workers.

The enterprise that is a monopsonist in the factor market may be a pure competitor in the product market. The isolated coal mine

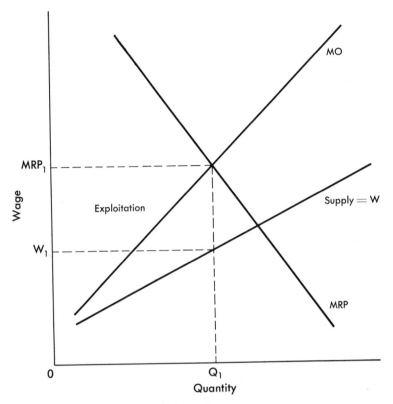

Figure 10-2.
Monopsony in the Labor Market

operator may set the wage of labor in his neighborhood, but he could scarcely set the price of coal for the whole market. Indeed, he may take the price of coal as set in the market. In that case he would have a perfectly elastic demand curve for his coal. He could sell all his output at the going price. The marginal revenue he receives for additional output would then equal the price. Where $P = MR$, the demand curve for labor (MRP) equals the value of the marginal physical product of labor (VMPP).

What wage will the monopsonist set? Or, to rephrase the question, how much labor will he hire? If he maximizes his profits, he will hire laborers up to the point where $MO = MRP$. He will hire laborers as long as additional laborers add more to revenue than to cost. In Figure 10-2 he will hire Q_1 laborers and pay them each W_1 in wages.

At the profit maximizing wage (W_1) labor is exploited, according to Joan Robinson's definition, because the wage of labor is below the VMPP of labor. The wage is also below the MRP of labor. Laborers are not paid the market value of what they create. They are paid something less. If the other firms in the product market pay competitive wages, the isolated firm enjoys excess profits equal to the area of exploitation shown in Figure 10-2. Since the firm operates in a purely competitive product market, all of this excess profit arises because of its monopsonistic power.

Monopsonistic exploitation on the buying side of the factor market can be offset by monopoly control of resources on the selling side of the factor market. If, for example, the miners who work in an isolated mining town were to form a union, they could press for higher wages. In Figure 10-2 they could demand and receive a wage equal to the VMPP of Q_1 workers. They could force the enterprise to pay the miners the full amount of exploited profits without reducing the employment of miners by one man. Indeed, if they asked for a wage between W_1 and $VMPP_1$, the quantity of laborers demanded would exceed the quantity employed in the absence of the union.

Monopolistic exploitation

Another type of resource exploitation occurs when an enterprise has monopolistic power in the product market, but not in the factor market. In this case, labor is paid less than the value of its marginal physical product (VMPP) because the demand for labor (MRP) is less than the VMPP of labor ($VMPP = P \times MP$, $MRP = MR \times MP$). The demand curve for a monopolist in the product market is downward sloping. If the monopolist wants to sell one more unit, he must lower the price on all the units he sells. As a result, the additional revenue (MR) he receives for selling one more unit is less than the price (P) of that unit. Thus, MRP is less than VMPP.

Monopolistic exploitation occurs even though the enterprise

has no control over the wages it pays. Even if the labor market is purely competitive and the enterprise takes the wage as set in the market, labor exploitation takes place. In Figure 10-3 it is assumed that the labor market is purely competitive. The firm can hire all the labor it wants at the going wage (MO = W). The firm maximizes its profits where MO = MRP. Up to that point the addition to revenue (MRP) exceeds the addition to cost (MO), and profits can be increased by hiring more laborers. Beyond that point the addition to cost (MO) exceeds the addition to revenue (MRP), and profits are reduced by hiring more laborers. At that point profits are maximized.

In equilibrium, the wage rate (W_1) is below the VMPP of labor. Thus, labor is exploited. This type of exploitation cannot be

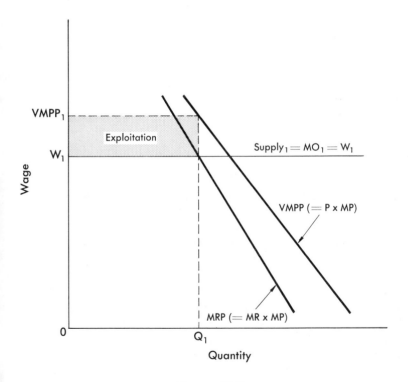

Figure 10-3.
Monopoly in the Product Market

eliminated by raising the wage rate. No matter how high the wage goes, the MRP curve is below the VMPP curve. As the wage rate rises, the firm will simply hire fewer and fewer laborers. Any excess profits that may be made in this situation are made because of the monopoly power which the firm has in the product market and not because of what happens in the labor market.

Limitations of the Marginal Productivity Theory

The marginal productivity theory is one of the least satisfactory branches of economic theory, particularly when it is applied to labor markets. The weaknesses of the theory are numerous, some of which are the following.

First, it is frequently difficult, if not impossible, to identify the marginal product of an additional laborer or group of laborers. This difficulty may arise because labor is often used in fixed proportions. What is the marginal product of the worker who installs carburetors on an automobile assembly line? His labor is indispensable. Yet his labor is certainly not the whole output of automobiles. He is part of a larger unit of production, and his contribution cannot easily be separated out. The automobile company demands the whole unit of production, and it pays the market or union scale.

Similarly, many firms have no identifiable unit of output. What is the marginal product of a lawyer, a policeman, a school teacher, a soldier, or a priest? Yet, there is a demand for these labor services.

Second, labor markets are very imperfect. Mobility is limited, in part, because people do not like to leave their homes, their friends, and familiar surroundings. People like to do the things they have always done, and frequently they prefer to remain in their home town at a low wage rather than leave at a high wage. Mobility is also limited, because knowledge of opportunities is limited. If people do not know where the greener pastures lie, they cannot find them. Where knowledge and mobility are imperfect, long-run tendencies may never work themselves out.

Third, standards of fairness, custom, and status influence the operation of labor markets. Everything is not a matter of profit and loss. Workers with seniority or with family responsibilities are often given preferential treatment. Workers are discriminated against because of their race, sex, religion, and national origin.

Fourth, many labor markets are unionized. In theory, unions are monopolies, but they often do not behave like monopolies. They do not maximize the wage of their members, or they do not maximize the income to their occupation. Many unions have spent millions of dollars trying to organize other unions, which may be of little or no economic advantage to the parent union. Other unions have established hospitals and other public institutions that serve union and nonunion people alike.

Finally, volumes and volumes of legislation influence the operation of labor markets. There are laws that permit unionization and laws that prohibit strikes. There are laws that set minimum wages, establish maximum hours, and forbid child labor. There are laws that provide for the public education of some workers and provide nothing for other workers. There are tax laws that give special treatment to owners of oil fields, family men, and clergymen. There are license laws that restrict the supply of school teachers, barbers, and doctors. All of these laws and more affect the operation of labor markets.

GLOSSARY

Cost: The expenditure in money, labor, or other resources necessary to produce or to acquire a good. A cost is an outlay, expenditure, price or sacrifice.

Average cost: The average cost of production is the total cost per unit of output. AC = TC ÷ Q. For example, if a total of $5,000 is spent on an automobile during its life—including the original price, taxes, licenses, gasoline, oil, tires, maintenance and repair—and if the car travels 50,000 miles during its life, the average cost is 10¢ per mile.

Fixed costs: Fixed costs do not vary with output. For example, the cost of an automobile license is a fixed cost which does not vary with the number of miles travelled.

Marginal cost: Marginal cost is the addition to total cost associated with an increase in output or the reduction in total cost associated with a decrease in output. Marginal cost is the additional, extra, incremental, or differential cost of increasing output.

$$MC = \frac{\text{change in TC}}{\text{change in Q}}$$

For example, the marginal cost of driving a car from New York to Boston is the expenditure on gasoline and oil plus the extra wear and tear on the car and the driver.

Opportunity cost: Opportunity cost is the cost of alternatives foregone. Since it is not possible to do everything, many things must be sacrificed for everything that is done. The opportunity cost of doing anything is the alternatives which could have been done instead. For example, to the student, the opportunity cost of studying economics is what could have been studied instead.

Total cost: The total cost of production is the sum of all expenditures incurred in producing a given volume of output. Total cost includes the cost of materials, labor, taxes, advertising, plant and equipment; it conventionally includes a "normal" profit which must be paid to the entrepreneur to induce him to organize production.

Variable cost: Variable costs vary with the volume of output. For example, the expenditure on gasoline increases as the number of miles travelled in an automobile increases.

Demand: The demand for a good is the alternative quantities purchasers are willing to buy at different prices. Consumers demand the goods produced by enterprises, and enterprises demand the factors of production.

Derived demand: The demand for factors of production is derived from the demand for the output which they produce.

Excess demand: An excess demand exists when the quantity demanded exceeds the quantity supplied at a given price. A rise in price will generally eliminate an excess demand.

Law of demand: The law of demand states: the higher the price, the smaller the quantity demanded; the lower the price, the greater the quantity demanded—provided the other variables which alter demand are constant.

Elasticity: Elasticity measures the responsiveness of the quantity demanded (or supplied) of a good to changes in its price, the price of other goods, or income.

Cross elasticity: The cross elasticity of demand relates the percentage change in the quantity demanded of one good to the percentage change in the price of another good.

$$\text{Cross elasticity} = \frac{\text{Percentage change in quantity of A}}{\text{Percentage change in price of B}}$$

Income elasticity: Income elasticity of demand relates the percentage change in the quantity demanded of a good to the percentage change in consumer income.

$$\text{Income elasticity} = \frac{\text{Percentage change in quantity of A}}{\text{Percentage change in consumer income}}$$

Price elasticity: Price elasticity (or direct elasticity) of demand relates the percentage change in the quantity demanded of a good to the percentage change in its price.

$$\text{Price elasticity} = \frac{\text{Percentage change in quantity of A}}{\text{Percentage change in price of A}}$$

Equilibrium: A market is in equilibrium when the quantity supplied equals the quantity demanded. Market forces push the quantity supplied and the quantity demanded into equilibrium. If the market is temporarily not in equilibrium, it will tend to return to equilibrium.

Exploitation: A factor of production is exploited if it receives less than the value of its marginal physical product (VMPP).

Factors of Production: The factors of production are land, labor, and capital. Entrepreneurship is sometimes counted as a fourth factor. Together, these factors produce the total output of society, and the total income of society is divided among these four factors in the form of rent, wages, interest, and profit.

Good: A good is anything that is capable of satisfying a want, requirement, or desire. Goods that are scarce relative to the demand for them have a market value, and are called economic goods. Goods that are so abundant that they have no price are called free goods, e.g., air.

Complementary goods: Two goods are complements if a rise in the price of one decreases the quantity demanded of both. For example, a rise in the price of beer might reduce the quantity of pretzels (as well as beer) which is demanded.

Differentiated good: A good is differentiated if, for any reason, consumers prefer it to its substitutes. For example, branded goods are differentiated.

Homogeneous good: A group of goods is homogeneous if they are identical, if there is no reason to prefer one over another.

Inferior good: A good is inferior if the quantity of it demanded decreases as consumer incomes increase. For example, as the income of consumers rises, they may buy fewer potatoes.

Substitute goods: Two goods are substitutes if a rise in the price of one increases the quantity demanded of the other. For example, a rise in the price of Chevrolets might increase the number of Fords which are demanded.

Income: Income is the proceeds from the sale of goods. The income of an enterprise is what it receives from the sale of its output, and the income of resource owners is the wages, rent, interest, or profit they receive from the sale of their factor services.

Income distribution: Income distribution refers to the way in which the total income generated from production is divided among the factors of production and among the population.

Income effect: When the price of a good changes, the real income of the demander or supplier is changed. The income effect is the effect produced on the quantity of a good which is demanded or supplied by the change in real income caused by a change in price.

Real income: The real income of a man is what his money income will buy in real goods and services. For example, the real income of a man who receives a 5% raise in his wages in a year during which prices rise 10% has actually fallen because, at the end of the year, he can buy less in real goods and services than he could buy at the beginning of the year.

Input: An input is a good used in the production of another good. The factors of production are inputs. For example, iron ore, coal, limestone, and labor are among the inputs used in the production of steel.

Laws of Production: Laws of production describe the interrelationships of physical inputs and outputs. There are four laws of production: (1) the law of diminishing returns, (2) the principle of factor substitution, (3) production possibilities, and (4) returns to scale.

Law of diminishing returns: The law of diminishing returns relates an input to an output. The law states that, as successive units of a variable input are taken into production, output will eventually increase at a diminishing rate, assuming at least one other input is fixed and assuming that the method of production (technology) does not change.

Principle of factor substitution: The principle of factor substitution describes how various combinations of inputs can be used to produce a constant output. Factor substitution is subject to a kind of diminishing returns: as successive units of one input are added to production, another input can only be withdrawn from production at a diminishing rate if output is to remain unchanged.

Production possibilities: The production possibilities curve of an enterprise describes the maximum output of one product which is possible, given various quantities of another product when the quantity of inputs is given. The substitution of outputs is subject to diminishing returns: equal decreases in the output of one product only release enough resources to produce diminishing rates of increase in the output of another product, provided a constant quantity of productive resources is used.

Returns to scale: The returns to scale of an enterprise describe what happens to the output of an enterprise when all its inputs vary in the same proportion. Returns to scale may increase, decrease, or remain constant.

Long Run: The long run is the length of time needed to adjust productive capacity to the most profitable level. In the long run all inputs can be varied. New plants can be constructed and old plants worn out.

Marginal Productivity Theory: The marginal productivity theory explains the demand for factors of production.

Marginal product: The marginal product (MP) of a factor of production is the change in total output associated with a change in the quantity of that factor which is used in production, assuming other inputs are constant.

$$MP = \frac{\text{Change in output}}{\text{Change in input}}$$

Marginal revenue product: The marginal revenue product (MRP) of a factor is the demand for that factor. It is the marginal revenue which a marginal factor can earn for an enterprise. $MRP = MR \times MP$. For example, if an additional laborer can produce an additional 5 units of output (MP) for an enterprise and if the enterprise can increase its revenue (MR) by $1.00 a unit when it sells that output, the enterprise will demand the laborer if the wage rate is $5.00 or less.

Value of the marginal physical product: The value of the marginal physical product (VMPP) of a factor of production is the amount for which the marginal product (MP) of that factor sell in the market. $VMPP = P \times MP$. Under pure competition, $VMPP = MRP$, because $P = MR$.

Marginal Utility Theory: The marginal utility theory explains the demand for consumer goods. To any particular consumer, the demand for a good is determined by the additional utility or satisfaction that an additional unit of that good gives the consumer. Since the marginal utility of a good declines as consumers acquire additional units of the good, the amount that consumers are willing to pay for additional units of a good declines. Thus, demand follows the law of demand.

Market: A market is any place or area in which a group of buyers and sellers regularly come into contact with one another to transact business. A market is where contracts are made.

Factor market: A factor market is a market in which resource owners sell and enterprises buy land, labor, and capital—the factors of production.

Product market: A product market is a market in which enterprises sell their output.

Market conduct: The market conduct of a firm (industry) is the policies which it follows, e.g., pricing policy, advertising policy, employment policy.

Market performance: The market performance of an industry (firm) refers to how well it serves society. How are resources allocated? How is income distributed? How progressive is the industry?

Market structure: The structure of a market is the environment in which buyers and sellers find themselves. The major elements of market structure define the competitive environment of a market: the number of buyers and sellers, the differentiation of the product, and the barriers to entry.

Monopolistic Competition: A monopolistically competitive market (1) contains so many buyers and sellers that they do not recognize their mutual dependence, (2) each enterprise sells a slightly differentiated product, and (3) buyers and sellers are free to enter into or exit from the market.

Monopoly: A monopoly is a market with only one seller. In the purest sense, a monopolist faces no competition at all. However, the term is also used to describe a market in which there is relatively little competition.

Monopsony: A monopsony is a market with a single buyer.

Oligopoly: An oligopoly is a market that contains so few sellers that they recognize their interdependence. The product may be homogeneous or differentiated. Entry may be easy or difficult.

Output: An output is a good which an enterprise produces and sells.

Price: The price of a good is what is exchanged for it. Prices are usually expressed as so much money per unit. Input prices include wage rates, interest rates, and rental rates.

Price discrimination: Price discrimination exists when different prices are charged for the same good in the same market.

Price theory: Price theory explains the way in which resources are allocated and income is distributed.

Relative price: The relative price of a good is the ratio at which it is exchanged for other goods. For example, if steel costs 5¢ a pound and aluminum costs 25¢ a pound, the relative price a pound of steel is one fifth of a pound of aluminum.

Reservation price: The reservation price of a seller is the price below which he will not sell, and the reservation price of a buyer is the price above which he will not buy.

Profit: Profit equals total revenue minus total cost. Profit = TR − TC.

Excess profit: An entrepreneur earns an excess profit when he earns more in one business than he can earn in his next best alternative. When excess profits are earned in one industry, entrepreneurs tend to enter that industry. Excess profits are sometimes called pure profits, or economic profits.

Normal profit: A normal profit is the minimum profit which can be paid to an entrepreneur to induce him to stay in business in the long run. When normal profits are earned in an industry there is no tendency for the number of firms in the industry to increase or decrease. Normal profits are conventionally considered to be a cost of production.

Profit maximization: Business enterprises are assumed to maximize their profits because they are in business for a profit. Profits are maximized when total revenue exceeds total cost by the greatest possible amount, when MR = MC, or when MRP = MO.

Pure Competition: A purely competitive market structure has three characteristics. (1) There are so many buyers and sellers that no one of them can significantly affect the market price. (2) All the enterprises produce and sell identical or homogeneous products. (3) Buyers and sellers are free to enter or leave the market.

Resource Allocation: Resource allocation refers to the way in which the scarce resources of an economy are allocated among competing goals. Every economy has limited quantities of land, labor, and capital, but unlimited uses for these resources. The profit motive directs the allocation of resources in a capitalistic economy.

Revenue: The revenue of an enterprise is its sales, receipts, or income.

Average revenue: The average revenue derived from selling a good is the same as the price at which it sells. $AR = TR \div Q = (P \times Q) \div Q = P$. The average revenue curve is the same as the demand curve for the output of a firm.

Marginal revenue: Marginal revenue is the change in total revenue associated with a change in the quantity sold.

$$MR = \frac{\text{Change in total revenue}}{\text{Change in quantity sold}}$$

For example, if a monopolist cut his price from $11 to $10 a unit and increased the quantity sold from 1,000 to 2,000 units, marginal revenue equals $9 per unit—$20,000 [(= $10 \times 2000) − $11,000 (= $11 \times 1000)] \div 1000 = $9.

Total revenue: Total revenue is the sum of all sales, receipts, or income of an enterprise. Total revenue equals the price times the quantity sold. $TR = P \times Q$.

Short Run: In the short run, at least one input is fixed. Plant and equipment is usually assumed to be fixed.

Substitution Effect: When the relative price of two goods changes, consumers tend to substitute the good which has become cheaper for the good which has become more expensive in order to maintain the level of satisfaction they derive from their income.

Supply: The supply of a good is the alternative quantities offered for sale at different prices. Resource owners supply the factors of production to enterprises which supply products to consumers.

Excess supply: An excess supply exists when the quantity supplied exceeds the quantity demanded at a given price. A fall in price will generally eliminate an excess supply.

Law of supply: The law of supply states that the higher the price, the greater the quantity supplied; the lower the price, the smaller the quantity supplied—provided the other factors which alter supply remain constant.

INDEX